TEACHING POETRY

ALSO BY JAMES REEVES

Collected Poems 1929–1959
The Questioning Tiger
Subsong

CRITICAL EDITIONS OF FOLK-SONG TEXTS

The Idiom of the People
The Everlasting Circle

ANTHOLOGIES

The Poets' World
The Modern Poets' World
The Speaking Oak
A New Canon of English Poetry (with Martin Seymour-Smith)

SELECTIONS IN THE POETRY BOOKSHELF SERIES

D. H. Lawrence
John Donne
Gerard Manley Hopkins
John Clare
Robert Browning
S. T. Coleridge
Emily Dickinson
Andrew Marvell (with Martin Seymour-Smith)

ABOUT POETRY

A Short History of English Poetry
The Critical Sense (practical criticism of prose and poetry)
Understanding Poetry
Inside Poetry

BY MARTIN SEYMOUR-SMITH

SELECTIONS IN THE POETRY BOOKSHELF SERIES

Shakespeare's Sonnets
Longer Elizabethan Poems

POETRY

Tea with Miss Stockport (Abelard-Schuman)
Reminiscences of Norma (Constable)

ABOUT POETRY

Poets Through their Letters (Constable)

JAMES REEVES

Teaching Poetry

POETRY IN CLASS
FIVE TO FIFTEEN

HEINEMANN
LONDON

Heinemann Educational Books Ltd
LONDON EDINBURGH MELBOURNE TORONTO
SINGAPORE JOHANNESBURG HONG KONG
NAIROBI AUCKLAND IBADAN
NEW DELHI

ISBN 0 435 14762 5

Published by
Heinemann Educational Books Ltd
48 Charles Street, London WIX 8AH

Printed in Great Britain by
Butler & Tanner Ltd
Frome and London

TO STELLA

Contents

INTRODUCTION   ix

PART I   THE TREES

Chapter 1   Choosing Poems   1

Chapter 2   Methods in General   11

Chapter 3   Infants and Younger Juniors (5–8)   30

Chapter 4   Juniors (8–11)   45

Chapter 5   The Secondary School: First Stage (11–13)   59

Chapter 6   The Secondary School: Second Stage (13–15)   71

PART II   THE WOOD

Chapter 7   Why Teach Poetry?   87

Chapter 8   'The Holy Incantation'   95

INDEX OF POETS AND POEMS   105

GENERAL INDEX   108

Acknowledgements

THE AUTHOR and publishers wish to thank the following for their permission to quote copyright material in this book: Mrs H. M. Davies and Messrs Jonathan Cape Limited, for *The Rabbit* from *The Collected Poems of W. H. Davies*; Mr Robert Graves for *A Cough*; the Literary Trustees of Walter de la Mare and Messrs Faber & Faber Limited for *The Old Tailor*, *Five Eyes* and '*Sooeep*'; the Trustees of the Hardy Estate and Messrs Macmillan & Co. Limited for *Weathers* from *Collected Poems* and *We be the King's Men* from *The Dynasts*; Messrs Constable & Co. Limited for *At Fifteen I Went with the Army* and *Madly Singing in the Mountains* from *170 Chinese Poems* by Arthur Waley; Mr Clive Sansom and Messrs A. & C. Black Limited for *Lightships* and *Clocks and Watches* from *Speech Rhymes Book II*; the Estate of the late Mrs Frieda Lawrence for an extract from *Hymns in a Man's Life* by D. H. Lawrence.

Introduction

ONE of the most serious handicaps which teachers have had to undergo during my time is inspirational writing—and speaking. In text-books of education, in addresses at Training Colleges, and from·Speech Day platforms they have been subjected to a current of hot air unknown to any other profession; beneath it any but the most robust constitution must wilt, especially on meeting the draught of cold reality which blows through the class room. If teachers tend in middle age to become disillusioned, it is partly owing to the atmosphere of inspiration in which they began their careers.

About the time I began teaching, it was possible for an international figure, noted as a philosopher-statesman, to address a centre of higher learning in these terms:

> The vision of freedom, of the liberation of the human spirit from its primeval bondage is perhaps the greatest light which has yet dawned on our human horizon. It forms the real spur of progress, the lure of our race in its ceaseless striving towards the future.[1]

I don't know whether a speaker in a similar situation could get away with that kind of thing nowadays; but every young teacher must be familiar with the vague, high-minded platitudes which fill the hardened listener with despair and the novice with a dangerous sense of unwarranted elation.

The trouble is that it is all meant for the best. Ideals we must have. Most of us need a sense of vocation, of purpose, or at least of direction if the daily routine is not to become meaningless. The difficulty is to see both the wood and the trees. The wood is the whole of education—the complex of processes by which an unschooled infant is gradually turned into a literate,

[1] General Smuts: Rectorial Address to St. Andrews University, 1934.

and to whatever degree mature, adolescent. Few teachers have time to think much about the wood while they are involved in it. The trees are the day-to-day business of class room instruction. A good many teachers are content to occupy themselves exclusively with this side of the business, and may be the more effective on that account.

During my years as a teacher I was much concerned with both the wood and the trees. For this reason I doubt if I was as good a teacher as I might have been; yet I was never satisfied with the day-to-day task unless I could work out for myself its ultimate purpose in the wider context. My chief interest became the teaching of poetry, about which I thought continually, and sometimes wrote. I was not happy about the state of poetry teaching generally, so far as I had contact with it. This book is the result—modest enough, it seems to me, considering it as a whole—of these years of reflection. I doubt if the practised teacher will find much in it that he has not found out for himself; my main hope is that the beginner will gain some understanding of a peculiarly difficult department of teaching.

Very many who have to teach poetry, especially in Modern Schools, are necessarily non-specialists. It is with them in mind that I have put the trees before the wood. I hope that I have managed to reduce the inspirational part of this book to a minimum, though I admit that early influences have been strong. At any rate I have kept it in decent obscurity at the end of the volume; thus the teacher who simply wants to get on with his job, and is glad of some practical suggestions, will find it easy to ignore what does not interest him.

I have limited my recommendations to the years of compulsory schooling, because after that period certain special considerations operate. The teaching of poetry during the G.C.E. years is in practice conditioned entirely by the demands of the examination. This is not the place to discuss the controversial question of 'set books', and I have no useful suggestions to make about how to pass a public examination in poetry. The reading of poetry in the Sixth Form is also too specialized to be dealt with here; I have treated it very fully elsewhere.[1]

This is, in short, a book for non-specialists; it gives a comprehensive account of the ways in which, after experience and reflection, I think poetry should be taught as a class room subject between the ages of five and fifteen.

Acknowledgements are due to the Editor of *The Use of English* in which parts of this book first appeared.

J.R.

Chalfont St Giles
1958

[1] *The Critical Sense* (Heinemann), 1956.

PART I

The Trees

CHAPTER I

CHOOSING POEMS

IN the teaching of any subject there are four factors to be considered: the pupil; the material to be taught; the methods adopted; and the personality of the teacher—using the word 'personality' in its broadest sense. In the following pages we shall consider all four factors, and more especially the second and third—material and method. For a teacher must take his pupils as he finds them: children of different kinds will need different methods, and to some extent different material. To study the needs of different children is a life's work. All that can be said here is that the best teacher is the one who is most successful in this continuous awareness of the varying needs of different children, and of the same children at different times. The problem is one which will concern us in these pages only incidentally, and in general terms. In speaking of 'the children', or 'the class' being taught, we shall be assuming an average— an average that never quite occurs in reality.

In teaching subjects such as Mathematics, where a high degree of instruction, as distinct from education, has to be done, the variable element in this average is less important: in other words, Mathematics must be taught as if all the pupils are capable of assimilating, and profiting from, a generally agreed syllabus of factual knowledge and calculating skill. This is not to imply that Mathematics can be taught mechanically. But it will generally be agreed that in teaching an aesthetic subject, such as Poetry, the differing personalities of children enter more largely into our calculations: so also do those other variables, the material chosen and the personality of the teacher. For the body of English poetry which forms an indispensable part of any syllabus is very small; there is a large body of poetry which *may* be taught, and very little that everyone would agree *must* be taught. Moreover, the factor of the teacher's personality is of added importance in the teaching of Poetry. To teach Mathematics or, to take another subject, Grammar—any mainly instructional subject, that is—makes less demand on the teacher's personality than to teach an aesthetic subject. To draw on my own experience, I always found, as an English teacher, that to take Grammar was a relief after taking Poetry; the demand on the intelligence of the teacher is no less, but the demand on his personality is much smaller. Poetry or Musical Appreciation—any subject where the emotions, the sense of discrimination, are involved—requires the continuous exercise of tact and skill in a way which Grammar does not. One may teach the same rules of Grammar more or less in the same way over and over again; but somehow each time one teaches a poem, it is a new poem—or at any rate, the poem-teacher-class relation is a new one. There is no need to labour the point. It is enough to insist that the fourth of the factors I have mentioned—the teacher's personality—plays an especially important part in the teaching of poetry.

Much will be said later about method, and about material. But since the factor of personality can be discussed only in general terms, it had better be considered briefly here. By 'personality' is meant, not only those elements of taste, judgement and training which determine a teacher's choice of material and attitude to Poetry, but also the impact he makes on the class when handling the subject. For where an aesthetic subject is concerned the lesson is always to some extent an essay in persuasion. The class must be persuaded to like what is good, or to find reasons for appreciating what it likes; a poetry lesson implies an effort to raise standards of taste.

Teaching poetry → persuading a likeness + appreciation.

There would be no point in devoting time and trouble to teaching children to like what they like already; even if we start with what they know and like, we cannot progress without extending the range of their appreciation to cover material that is new to them and—in some degree, however slight— more difficult to appreciate than what they know already.

A teacher who is enthusiastic about what he is teaching, and persuasive in his methods, can achieve immense results in this direction. It is not necessary to be personally enthusiastic for Grammar in order to teach it successfully. But one who tries to teach the appreciation of an art without appreciating it himself is wasting time. He cannot succeed, except temporarily and in a very limited way, and his insincerity will be discovered, so that the most decisive result of his teaching will be a distaste for his subject on the part of the class—or at least boredom and apathy. Imagine a man who never went to a concert or listened to the radio or the gramophone trying to teach the appreciation of music! This is something that never occurs in practice, because music is regarded as a specialist's interest. Unfortunately, however, it does sometimes occur in the teaching of poetry, because poetry is only one branch of the subject known by the portmanteau name of 'English'. It is no exaggeration to say that many teachers of English, though they may be skilled instructors in grammar and composition, and enthusiastic exponents of fiction, the essay, and the drama, yet have no deep personal love of poetry—have long since given up trying to write it themselves, if they ever did, and never open a book of poems for their own recreation. This is not an attack on English teachers—goodness knows, enough is expected of them in the way of a variety of assorted knowledge and skills, and if an English teacher can teach grammar, show how to write an essay or a précis, arouse interest in *The Pilgrim's Progress*, *David Copperfield*, and *Travels with a Donkey*, besides perhaps supervising the school library and magazine and the annual school play, one can admit that he is pretty well equipped. It is not to be expected that his training and tastes are such that he is also an enthusiast for poetry. This is an unpoetic age—the taste for poetry is not widespread, and those days are long past when an educated man was expected to know something of his nation's poets. Perhaps the remedy would be to appoint specialists in poetry, though education authorities might well shrink from having poetry advisers, as well as drama and music advisers. Yet poetry is far more neglected than these two other arts.[1]

Without pursuing this discouraging train of thought further, it is only to be hoped that as many teachers as possible will be able to bring to the teaching of poetry at least some enthusiasm for some of the poetry that children can appreciate. One thing must be admitted—the enthusiast is not necessarily a born teacher: to possess an enthusiasm is one thing, to infect others with it is another. All the same, the teacher's personal enjoyment of poetry is a cardinal element in success.

The other vital element is the teacher's discrimination, his personal taste. For, since without enthusiasm poetry cannot be taught, it follows that *with* enthusiasm bad poetry can be taught as successfully as good. To put it baldly, the better a teacher is, and the worse his taste, the more harm he is doing! It must be insisted on, from the start, that, in the long run, a teacher's taste —his judgement of poetic quality—is more important by far than the methods he uses and the persuasive skill at his command. For so long as a teacher is sure of his personal standards in this vital matter, and is determined to compromise them as little as possible, then he can go as far as he likes towards meeting the interests and tastes of his pupils; and provided he is teaching a good poem, it does not really matter how he teaches it, so long as in the end some of the class—most of it, perhaps— enjoy the poem better than they did at first. Once this has been said, it can be admitted that an impeccable taste combined with a dull and uninspiring class technique and a total ignorance of

[1] In the Index to the *B.B.C. Handbook for 1956* the number of page-references under the heading 'Music' is 44, under the heading 'Drama' 23, and under the heading 'Poetry' 2.

what is suitable for a particular group of children would be useless. But in practice the two never go together. One can hardly conceive of an enthusiast for Donne's *Elegies* who is so misguided as to try to teach them to a class of eight-year-olds. Yet this may be a preferable form of lunacy to plodding along with some worthless doggerel because it happens to be within the children's grasp.

There is a defeatist tag to the effect that there is no disputing about tastes. It is true that there is never final agreement about tastes, but for this very reason there *is*, and always will be, dispute. Even if I could, I would not, hand to a would-be poetry teacher a list of what I considered the best English poems and say 'These are what you must try to like'. Taste must come from within. It can be caught from a speaker, a teacher, or from books; it can be self-taught by reading and considering. To take one or two simple illustrations: the knowledge of what constitutes a good stroke at cricket or tennis, or good style in boxing, or a good car design, comes naturally to those who constantly study sport or motoring—it can be increased by reading books and by discussion with others. But its basis is personal acquaintance with the subject, a habit of thought and reflection and comparison. It is this training which enables the expert, or the enthusiast, to reject what is inferior and prefer the best. The same is true of taste in the arts, except that they are enormously more complicated and more subjective: in the arts, emotion is involved as it is not in sport or in car design. Where emotion is involved, personal considerations enter to distort or reinforce judgement. It is possible for private reasons to dislike all poems about war, or love, or religion; it is equally possible to overvalue such poems, purely on account of their subject-matter. Yet the more one reads and reflects on poetry, the more does one's judgement become independent of such personal considerations; so that, though one may recognize that one prefers, say, religious poems to love poems, one can tell the difference between a good love poem and a bad one.

To decide what are good poems for children, one should apply the same criteria as for poetry in general, except that one must try to read it with the understanding, the vocabulary, and the feelings of a child. The idea that there is a kind of poetry inferior to the poetry that adults appreciate but which is all right for the young is, to my mind, the heresy which has done most to turn children away from poetry. The appreciative powers of children may be more limited than ours—especially when it comes to mature or adult emotions—but they deserve and need poetry of as high aesthetic quality. To take an example: we, as adults, may feel that we have grown out of the simple, martial, patriotic emotions which can make Macaulay's *Horatius* a thrilling experience to boys. But of its kind *Horatius* is not a bad poem: its style is clear-cut, vigorous and economical; its tone healthy. The heroics, though crude, are not overdone, and there is nothing sensational or jingoistic. History is no doubt simplified, and human nature reduced to a few clearly-defined emotions. Nevertheless, it is, of its kind, a poem in good taste, written with conviction and some narrative skill. There is nothing in it unworthy of a teacher's attention who is looking for something stirring and memorable for the average boy of about twelve. It is not inferior in *quality* to some of the poems we enjoy as adults; it is simply of another kind. If we have grown out of it, that is because we have grown out of the mental attitudes and the emotional outlook we possessed at the age of twelve.

This is not to say that Macaulay represents the height of achievement in poetry suitable for children. Yet its qualities of vigour and directness are those we find also in poetry of much greater imaginative power—Border ballads, for instance, such as *Sir Patrick Spens*, in which the conflict of human passions and its attendant tragedy are of an altogether higher order. *Sir Patrick Spens* is also of a much greater economy of expression than *Horatius*, which contains a good deal of rhetorical repetition. The virtue of economy, combined with vigour and directness, is conspicuous in the best folk-rhymes and songs, as well as in the so-called nursery rhymes taught orally to infants. Another element in poetry suitable for children is rhythmic vitality. The best folk-songs and ballads move boldly and energetically from line to line and from verse to verse, without the mechanical deadness which betrays the imitation ballad writing of later times. *John Gilpin* has for this reason always seemed to me boring, and I have never known a child feel any enthusiasm for it, although it recurs with monotonous regularity in school anthologies. But this may be a deficiency of taste on my part. Certainly, *John Gilpin* is a better poem than *How they Brought the Good News from Ghent to Aix*, though Browning is superior to Cowper in so many respects. *How they Brought the Good News* is a piece of youthful high spirits on the part of a man who loved riding; but this does not excuse its geographical inaccuracy, the obscurity of its narrative, and its sentimental view of horses.

Truth of feeling and appropriateness of language are the main criteria in choosing lyrical poetry. It is sometimes said that children cannot appreciate lyrics. Even if this were true, it would not excuse teachers from trying to extend the range of their experience by getting them to read lyrics. For the experience in narrative poems is comparatively specialized; lyrics are concerned more directly and exclusively with feelings—gladness or sorrow, regret, excitement, fear, love, anger or—the most universal emotion of immature humanity—delight in creation. The great value of lyrics for children is that they make these feelings articulate; they help children to experience the world with heightened sensibilities. To enjoy, say, Nashe's *Spring, the sweet spring* is to get more pleasure from spring itself. It is for the teacher to choose those lyrics which seem most sincere, most spontaneous, most vivid and vital. To think of a handful of lyrics by Christina Rossetti, Blake, Shakespeare, Walter de la Mare, Tennyson and Hardy is to realize, not indeed that poetry is indispensable to life, but certainly that life would be less full and rich, and the world less wonderful and less exciting, without them.

We are not concerned in this chapter with general principles, and it is not proposed at present to go into greater detail
in naming poets and poems; but it is worth adding that variety
not only of subject is to be sought, but also of form and mood.
Not only ballads and songs, rhymes and lyrics, must be chosen;
but also humorous and nonsensical poems, like those of Lear;
religious poems, such as carols and psalms; poems with refrains
and choruses, poems in free verse, like Arthur Waley's Chinese
translations; and for older pupils, sonnets, blank verse, satire,
parody. It is one of the great merits of poetry, for educational
purposes, if we can take advantage of it, that it is as various as
life itself—indeed, much more various than most lives. Poetry
is, indeed, life itself as it is lived at the fullest, distilled into
words and experienced through words. When we consider
all that good poetry contains, we realize that there is no time
for what is second-rate, imitative, feeble, lacking in vitality.
No one would claim that the poems of Edward Lear are of the
same value as Blake's, but of their kind they are supremely
good; and in teaching poetry we need all kinds. The kind of
poem to avoid is the pale imitation whether of Blake or of
Lear—the sentimental animal poem on the one hand, or the
trivial facetious jingle on the other.

Let us, in conclusion, consider a question often asked, in one
form or another: to what extent should a teacher be guided in
his choice of poems by the consideration of what the children
like? Any teacher accused of taking up the time of his class
with inferior material nearly always answers, 'Well, they like
it.' There are two reasonable answers to this comment,
apparently contradictory but in reality complementary. First
it doesn't matter whether they like it or not so long as it is
good; and second, of course, they ought to like all the poems
they read—otherwise there would be no point in reading them.
Now there is a certain amount of confusion here. The teacher
on the defensive, if pressed, would not seriously maintain that
children should be allowed to read something in class *merely*
because they like it. Otherwise they might as well stick to

comics, and there's an end of it. Moreover, what do we mean by 'like'? Are we so sure that they know that they like? The expression 'they like it' may mean no more than that 'it' is familiar and they object to it less than to something else. Again, we are justified in asking, 'At what stage do they like it? Perhaps they already liked it before the teacher began teaching it, and he has in fact been simply indulging a taste they have unthinkingly formed of their own accord. There may be no harm in this, but there is not much good.' Surely if a class already likes something, the good teacher will want to extend the range of their appreciation to something that is so far unfamiliar and therefore as yet unliked. He should be thinking, not of what they already enjoy, but of what they should go on to enjoy further.

Whether a class will enjoy a new poem depends as much as anything on how it is taught. Something that seems to have no attraction for them at first hearing may, after they have worked at it, become a permanent possession. A diet exclusively of what they already like, without effort, will in the end cloy.

When all is said, however, it must be admitted that there are certain subjects in poetry which have more appeal than others. Narrative poems of action go down better with boys of nine to fourteen years old than most other kinds of poem. Love poems may be disliked by school-children not only because they are often badly taught, but also because the subject is embarrassing. It is all a matter of suiting the poem to the child. This is not in the least the same as saying that we must lower our standards for children. It means, rather, that we must continually study the nature and interests of the children, their emotional development, their maturity or immaturity of outlook, their range of vocabulary and intelligence; then out of our stock of available poems of good quality and varied kinds we can choose those which best suit a particular class at a particular time. In certain schools in certain districts all poetry may be unacceptable: perhaps the teaching has been bad; perhaps the local atmosphere is philistine and unsympathetic. Then the task of the poetry teacher is hard, though never absolutely impossible; for amidst the great wealth of English poetry there *are* songs to soothe the savage breast, if we know where to find them. The discriminating teacher will not choose lyrics of subtle verbal perfection and delicacy of expression, he will begin with the hearty, boisterous songs of sailors and tramps and cowboys, full of humour, crude feeling and strongly marked rhythm. There need be no sacrifice of quality here, only a careful limitation of theme and emotional range; I doubt if any English children can resist the appeal of such poems. After that, it will be the teacher's task, never easy but always fascinating, to extend his pupils' experience of poetry to include work of subtler form and maturer theme. The educative power of poetry is unlimited, if only we can discover how to choose rightly. Without the teacher's personal enthusiasm for his subject, the prospect is bleak; with enthusiasm, it is immense.

CHAPTER 2

METHODS IN GENERAL

AT the same time as a teacher is finding out what poems he can best read with particular classes, he must think about methods of teaching them. If all children came from literary homes and were possessed of the reading habit, it would only be necessary to place in their hands plenty of suitable material. Poetry would then teach itself. But in practice this does not happen. To the majority of children poetry must be taught; and how it is taught will make all the difference to their attitude towards it. To some extent this is true of all classroom subjects; and as with other subjects, so the main principles in devising methods of teaching poetry are two—liveliness and variety.

Yet this is especially true for poetry. With subjects such as Geography or Mathematics, factual content determines method; and although no one now believes that the teaching of any subject is best carried out by simply imparting a series of facts, yet it remains true that factual content is less influential in determining method with poetry than with perhaps any other subject. Let us put it this way: if we want to impart to a class some knowledge of the life of the Red Indians, we do not do this by reading with them Longfellow's *Hiawatha*. If we read *Hiawatha* at all, it will be for its poetic qualities. The same is true of anything else we read in the poetry lesson—Keats's odes, the Robin Hood ballads, or the lyrics of Wordsworth. It is not the factual content of these poems, the information they contain, which is the subject of the lesson—it is the poems themselves. This seems obvious, but it is often forgotten. I once heard a poetry lesson given to a class of nine-year-olds on Longfellow's *The Windmill*; and it soon became evident that what the master was teaching was not poetry but economic geography of a simple character: windmills, the grinding of corn, the making of bread, the use of bread, and so on till we ended up in the wheatlands of Canada, where the teacher was a good deal more at home than in the less easily defined regions of lyric poetry. We must be sure that when we teach poetry, it is poetry we are concerned with, not something else; the reading of a poem in class must not be aimed at imparting information—whether factual or narrative—it must be an experience, an active experience of poetry. The content of a poem—what it is about—is of importance only in relation to other qualities—qualities of form and language, of the poet's attitude to his subject. A poem may well be about the corn— or Red Indians—or cowboys—or wild flowers, but if the lesson is about these things and not about the poem, it is not an experience of poetry.

The character of liveliness in a poetry lesson is particularly important if we are to achieve the aim of making it an active experience. For the poetic experience has largely become a mental one: the original elements of dancing and music with which it was once associated have been all but lost. Undoubtedly it would be a very good thing if poetry could again be associated with singing, as once it was; but until teachers are differently educated and trained, and our whole conception of the relations between the various school subjects is revised, this must remain a Utopian idea. It is better to accept the notion of poetic experience as largely mental, and try not to let that fact make the poetry lesson over-intellectual, and too purely verbal.

A dancing lesson, a singing lesson, a craft lesson, even an art lesson, is by its nature more active than a poetry lesson. If poetry is to take its proper place among the arts in the school curriculum, everything must be done to make it active and lively.

The essential accompaniment to liveliness is variety. A poetry lesson in which the same poem is read in the same way throughout, cannot be called lively. No absolute rules can be laid down, but the liveliest lessons are likely to be those in which several poems of different moods are read, each in a different way—how many should be read in one lesson will depend on the length and character of the poems chosen, their difficulty, and the attitude of the class. It may be taken as a useful general rule that for every year in the age of a class, they will be interested in the same experience for not more than one and a half to two minutes. Under average conditions, that is to say, a teacher should not expect a class of seven-year-olds to be interested in the same poem for more than ten minutes or so. With such a class, if the lesson lasts for twenty minutes the teacher should try to deal with at least two poems—perhaps even three if one of them is no more than a simple speech-rhyme. With a class of fourteen-year-olds a teacher should be able to study the same poem for twenty minutes or more.

The poems chosen to be read in any lesson should be varied—either by a contrast with one another or by a difference in treatment. But above all, variety should be achieved by the choice of method.

Every poem requires a different treatment. This may dismay many teachers at the outset, though it is something which every good teacher of poetry discovers for himself. It is what makes the teaching of poetry one of the most interesting, though one of the most difficult of tasks. A Mathematics teacher may use a set procedure for solving simultaneous equations, a French teacher may tackle a piece of unseen translation according to certain unvarying rules, an English teacher may recommend a fixed method for writing a précis; but these things are logical exercises or disciplines, and uniformity is not harmful—indeed, it is probably helpful. But with the arts, uniformity is deadly. So it must be repeated, and kept constantly in mind, that every poem needs a different treatment.

The most important task for the teacher of Poetry, once he has decided to read a particular poem, is to study it by himself, at leisure, and determine what is its nature, its intention, its unique character. For every good poem is unique, and different from every other. If he reads the poem and thoroughly understands it—if he truly *knows* it—the poem itself will suggest the right way of teaching it—or *a* right way, since there may be more than one. Preparation of material is of the utmost importance. Any teacher who has gone into class unprepared knows this. The first part of his lesson is taken up with discovering what sort of a poem he has chosen, and by the time he has discovered this, the class may be puzzled or bored or at a loss to know what is expected of them. The good teacher is the one who prepares a number of poems for his class, gets to know them thoroughly, and so gradually builds up what might be called a repertoire of poems which he knows he can teach successfully—that is, he knows he can get the class to share his experience of them. Of course he will be continually adding to, or modifying his repertoire; he will be prepared for the situation which so often occurs: a poem which has gone well with, say, a first-year class for a number of years, fails to interest another class of the same age, for no apparent reason. No teacher, however experienced, can always be sure that any poem will succeed every time. Teaching poetry is a continuous process of trial and error, and anything approaching sureness of touch comes only after many failures.

Let us take one or two examples. It has been decided to read *The Song of the Western Men* with a class of nine-year-olds. If the class is all boys, or mixed, the choice is a good one: it is not necessarily such a good choice for a class of girls. This poem, it will be remembered, is by the Reverend Stephen Hawker, Vicar of Morwenstow in Cornwall, about the trial of the Seven Bishops in 1688. It is a noisy, vigorous poem mostly in direct speech, with a memorable refrain, in simple ballad metre.

> *A good sword and a trusty hand!*
> *A merry heart and true!*
> *King James's men shall understand*
> *What Cornish lads can do.*

And have they fixed the where and when?
　　And shall Trelawny die?
Here's twenty thousand Cornish men
　　Will know the reason why!

Out spake their captain brave and bold,
　　A merry wight was he:
'If London Tower were Michael's hold,
　　We'll set Trelawny free!

'We'll cross the Tamar, land to land,
　　The Severn is no stay,—
With "one and all",[1] and hand in hand,
　　And who shall bid us nay?

'And when we come to London Wall,
　　A pleasant sight to view,
Come forth! Come forth, ye cowards all,
　　Here's men as good as you!

'Trelawny he's in keep and hold,
　　Trelawny he may die;—
But here's twenty thousand Cornish bold
　　Will know the reason why!'

This is obviously not a poem for silent reading; it is simple, so that the class can perform it with little help from the teacher. There are few problems of vocabulary, but enjoyment will be increased by some knowledge of the historical background. It is here that the over-conscientious teacher will be tempted to give a history lesson; but the poem must be kept to the forefront and only sufficient history introduced to give the poem its setting. Of course it should be sung, rather than spoken, and in schools where this is done there will be a useful link between the poetry and the singing lesson. A poem such as this easily reveals its character and suggests a method of treatment. But the teacher who adopts a uniform method of, say, reading a

[1] The motto of Cornwall.

poem out loud himself, asking the class to explain difficult words, and then getting one or more of the class to repeat the poem, misses the opportunity of making this an active and lively experience. |Some poems require explanation, others do not. Sometimes it is well to write difficult words on the board before ever the poem is read; these can be explained, and the class will thus be prepared for their appearance in the poem, and their interest will not be suspended owing to lack of understanding. Sometimes, however, the vocabulary can be left to look after itself. |

Suppose it has been decided to read Shelley's sonnet *Ozymandias* with a fourteen-year-old class.

> I met a traveller from an antique land
> Who said: Two vast and trunkless legs of stone
> Stand in the desert. . . . Near them, on the sand,
> Half sunk, a shattered visage lies, whose frown,
> And wrinkled lip, and sneer of cold command,
> Tell that its sculptor well those passions read
> Which yet survive, stamped on these lifeless things,
> The hand that mocked them, and the heart that fed.
> And on the pedestal these words appear:
> 'My name is Ozymandias, king of kings:
> Look on my works, ye Mighty, and despair!'
> Nothing beside remains. Round the decay
> Of that colossal wreck, boundless and bare
> The lone and level sands stretch far away.

Here, although the sound of the poem is not unimportant, and something may be gained from an oral reading, this element is less vital. In *Ozymandias* an argument is worked out and presented through a visual experience; and it is here more important for the reader to be able to *see* the picture of ruin and desolation, and to comprehend intellectually and emotionally the significance of the words engraved on the statue's pedestal. It might, therefore, be appropriate in this case for the class first to read the poem silently, to see what they make of it. Possibly the vocabulary would need some elucidation; and, when the details have been thoroughly understood, the argument should be followed out and paraphrased, so that the intellectual content can be grasped. Again, however, the poem should not be made the occasion of a lesson in politics merely, or a discussion about the relative merits of democracy and tyranny: these things may well arise from the lesson. But the final impression left by the poem should be of an imaginative experience—an experience of the vanity of worldly power. Incidentally, *Ozymandias* is a poem which can legitimately call forth the reader's talent for drawing or painting. It is a visual as well as an intellectual experience, in a way in which *The Song of the Western Men* is not.

These examples could be multiplied indefinitely—indeed, to do so is an essential part of the teacher's task. I have not attempted to treat fully the question of how these examples should be tackled in class; I have tried merely to indicate the kind of method appropriate in each case. Every poem is different and must be taught differently. At the same time, certain broad distinctions can be indicated. It would be impossible for any teacher to re-think the whole of his practice for every poem.

The two main methods may be called critical and non-critical. *The Song of the Western Men*, since it is not hard to understand, can be taken 'straight'—that is, with only a minimum of explanation. Although the question of who Trelawny was, and the historical background generally, is interesting and should certainly be touched on, it is not vital to the appreciation of the poem as an experience. Provided the poem is read in a forthright, rousing manner, with conviction, the sense of local pride and independence which underlies it, will get through. This is the main thing. Indeed, to make too much of the background to the poem will weaken its impact. However, this is not a poem, perhaps, which is best read quite uncritically.

The first and most obvious non-critical method is for the teacher himself to read the poem, as he might read a story, for

B

recreation, with no comment whatever. So might *The Jumblies* be read to a class of eight-year-olds. I do not suggest that all critical comment on this poem would be irrelevant; but it is essentially a poem to enjoy uncritically and even unthinkingly. I take this opportunity of stressing the importance of the teacher's own reading, and of protesting most indignantly against the idea, still sometimes expressed, that a teacher who reads well to his class and asks nothing of them other than that they should listen is somehow not doing his job—not teaching. On the contrary, if more teachers would read really well—that is, convey the essential magic in a work of imagination through the medium of his voice and understanding—rather than perpetually talk about the matter in hand, ask questions, and worry a lot of answers out of the class, the teaching of literature would be much more effective. To read well needs a good voice, patience, understanding, some histrionic power, even some personality. How, then, can any teacher exercising these qualities be accused of not doing his job. My own first memorable experience of poetry was the reading of *Reynard the Fox* by a master who should have been teaching me Latin. He never asked questions about Masefield's poem, he never explained it, he simply read it—that is, he performed it. I made up later for the lost Latin, and the poetic experience was imperishable. The right to be read to is every child's birthright. His teacher may be the first person he ever meets who can read aloud effectively. Educationists rightly disapprove of lessons in which the teacher 'does all the talking'. But if he is reading poetry it is not he who is talking—it is Masefield, or Coleridge, or Lear, or our anonymous ancestors who composed *Sir Patrick Spens* and *Robin Hood and the Widow's Three Sons*. There is no higher role for an English teacher than to impersonate the poets—not always, perhaps, but often certainly.

While we are here concerned mainly with group methods of reading poetry, the value of silent reading should not be overlooked. This may be done either as a preparation for critical reading, or simply as recreation. There is no need to think that every poem has to be read aloud collectively. Obviously the more meditative kind of poem is suitable for silent reading. If the teacher intends to deal with the poem critically, then silent reading will often be a valuable preparation, and members of the class can be asked to say what they have made of the poem before the teacher gives his own view. Silent preparation will also be found useful as a preliminary to choral speaking. It is obvious that the younger the class, the less silent reading they should have; but even with quite young children an occasional ten minutes' silent reading will be a change from the perpetual sound of their own and their teacher's voices. In no other way can they train the inward ear, which is one important means of appreciating poetry.

The question of how far poems should be read aloud by individuals in the class is often asked. In this matter there may be a certain conflict of principles. All experience of poetry—and especially the first experience of a new poem—should be of high quality. Ideally, therefore, children should never hear an indifferent performance of a poem which the teacher hopes they will get to know and like. This is another of the important truths which are so often overlooked because they are obvious. First impressions are, if not everything, at any rate a great deal. Should the teacher, then, always be the one to introduce a new poem? Common sense, as well as regard for the children's wishes, suggests that this would be a mistake. Uniformity of method, in any case, is to be avoided. Nevertheless, I am sure that this would be better than to ask any child at random to read a new poem aloud to the whole class without preparation. Yet this is often done, and I am sure that it does much to spoil the attraction of poetry. A compromise seems to be indicated.

In the first place, the class should not have their books open while a poem is being read to them for the first time. It is not natural to follow in a book while someone is reading to you. The attention is divided between voice and print, and full concentration upon the poem cannot be achieved. If the teacher

full attention on the poem .

intends to read a new poem to the class, he should first produce an atmosphere of physical relaxation—there is much to be said for the 'arms folded on the desk' formula—combined with mental receptivity. The attitude required can perhaps best be described as one of negative expectancy—the minds of the children are alert, expecting something, but they do not know what. How such a mental attitude can be secured can only be discovered by every teacher for himself. Here, it must be enough to say that he will have little difficulty if the class have previously learnt to enjoy poetry and hence to approach a new experience of it with pleasurable anticipation. Eyes and ears should be focused on the reader alone. If the ears are on the teacher and the eyes on the book, the effect will be like that of reading the theatre programme while the curtain goes up on the play.

The same will hold good if the reader is one of the class. For this reason, I do not think it suitable for a pupil to read to the class while sitting or standing in his place. Whether he is at the back or the front, it is going to be hard for the others to focus their attention on him. He should come out and stand in front of the class, much as the teacher does. It is sometimes objected that this creates disturbance and wastes time. But unless the classroom is hopelessly over-furnished, this is not a serious problem; and the few seconds 'wasted' are part of the preparation for the poem.

The practice of 'reading round the class', or of allotting the several verses of a poem to several children, selected at random, is widespread and seems harmless. Moreover, it appears to be fairer than limiting the performers to the few best. It gives the weakest a chance. It seems to me to have the sanction of custom, but little else to recommend it. It should be felt that to read in front of the class is not only a privilege, but something the others can look forward to enjoying. They cannot do this if the reader is a poor one. Moreover, feelings of inferiority are bound to be heightened if poor readers are asked to give solo performances; for either their lack of skill will spoil the reading and be resented, however politely, or they will be so unskilled as to be passed over altogether. Now, every member of a class should have some training in reading. In a junior school there are set reading lessons. To mix this up with the appreciation of poetry is bad practice. So reading poetry aloud to the class should be reserved for the best readers, so long as it is understood that any child can qualify by making efforts with his reading. In my experience the class as a whole does not resent listening to only the best readers, provided they feel that these are chosen on grounds of merit, and not favouritism. A poetry lesson is something of a special occasion, like a school concert or a cricket match. No one resents not listening to a soprano solo by a child who is tone deaf, and no one expects the captain of the cricket team to put every boy on to bowl.

Having insisted on this, I must go on to add that it should be possible, given sufficient time, to let every member of the class have his turn as a soloist, even though there may be a few who perform oftener than the others. To make a child who is a bad reader perform publicly may permanently damage that child's self-confidence, especially perhaps if he feels that the rest of the class is being polite and making allowances. No, the teacher's aim must be to make every child a good enough reader to be able to read publicly. Undoubtedly the best method of doing this, apart from specific reading lessons, is the method of poetic appreciation known as Choral Speech.

Much has been written about Choral Speech, and no brief account is likely to be of much practical help to a teacher entirely unfamiliar with the method.[1] The steady growth of interest, however, has made practical courses a common feature of work in training colleges and of conferences of English teachers. Choral Speech may be defined briefly as the *organized* speaking of poetry aloud, or as *active* appreciation, or yet again as the acting of poetic form. It is entirely different from the old 'recitation' lessons on which older teachers were brought up.

[1] The best short account is the 80-page *An Approach to Choral Speech* (Macmillan, 1934) by Mona Swann, one of the pioneers of this method.

In these the pupil was expected to make a personal exhibition by saying a poem in accordance with preconceived standards of diction and expression laid down by the teacher. In Choral work the individual pupil acts as a member of a group—the group being a whole class, or a fraction of a class. Sometimes the class is divided into two equal groups, so that each group can hear, and criticize, the other's performance. Solo passages there may be, but these are not personal exhibitions, they are contributions to a group whole. Arbitrary methods of treating a poem are not laid down in advance; each poem is studied for itself, and the class or group, with or without help from the teacher, devises the method of presentation appropriate. With beginners the teacher will have to do much of the deciding; as the group gains in experience its members will take an increasing share in deciding on the best method of presentation.

The simplest method consists in a unison reading of the whole poem. This would be appropriate to, say, Hardy's *We be the King's Men, hale and hearty*, in which all the militia-men are supposed to be speaking all the time. But it soon appears that this method leads to monotony and is in any case suitable only for a limited number of poems. *We be the King's Men* has the refrain 'Right fol-lol', and clearly this might be spoken by a different body of speakers from those who say the rest of the poem. Perhaps, therefore, the better way would be to give the verses to a fairly large sub-chorus or semi-chorus, and let the whole group speak the refrain.

> We be the King's men, hale and hearty,
> Marching to meet one Buonaparty;
> If he won't sail, lest the wind should blow,
> We shall have marched for nothing, O!
>   Right fol-lol!

> We be the King's men, hale and hearty,
> Marching to meet one Buonaparty;

If he be sea-sick, says 'No, no!'
We shall have marched for nothing, O!
    Right fol-lol!

We be the King's men, hale and hearty,
Marching to meet one Buonaparty:
Never mind, mates; we'll be merry, though
We may have marched for nothing, O!
    Right fol-lol!

A poem of a slightly more elaborate form is *The Song of the Western Men*, already referred to.[1] While this also calls for a large group to represent the Cornish men, it would obviously be appropriate to allocate the Captain's words to a single speaker selected for vigour and clarity of speech, and a certain forthrightness of manner.

Poems in which a semi-chorus alternates with the whole group are some of the sea-shanties, such as *A Yankee Ship*, and here the alternation of question and answer indicates a further division into smaller groups.

The analysis of *Sir Patrick Spens* reveals the presence of certain solo speakers—the King, Sir Patrick, the elder knight and a member of Sir Patrick's crew—and of two main groups—the Scots lords (and ladies) and the Norwegian lords.

It is not proposed here to go into further detail on the subject of Choral Speech. The foregoing examples are some of the simplest methods of presentation, each of which suggests itself as a result of analysing the poem in question. It is wrong to adapt a poem to a predetermined method of presentation. Now if these suggestions come from the children themselves, it is clear that they must first have read and in some degree understood the poem. Often a class will initiate the most lively discussion of method without realizing that this is a form of indirect criticism. All that the younger children need to know of elementary literary criticism is learnt in the course of discussing how best to present a poem chorally. Moreover,

[1] See pp. 14-15.

Choral Speech discourages exhibitionism by subordinating the individual to the group presentation; and encourages shy children by making them speak poetry with the support of a chorus, by making suggestions when the class is at a loss, or by tactfully questioning the rightness of a suggestion which he feels to be mistaken. The great virtue of Choral Speech is that it is *active*; it involves hard and stimulating work by the class with the teacher as much as possible in the background. This makes for increased enjoyment. The danger with most methods is that the class is apt to be passive and the teacher too much to the fore.

Choral Speech, however, must not be allowed to degenerate into a 'stunt'. It must not be practised for its own sake, or for display, or for an exhibition of cleverness, but must always aim at making poetry more comprehensible, more real and more enjoyable. As an example of pointless elaboration, I may instance a reading of Hardy's *Weathers* I once heard, in which one speaker said the opening line and all the other long lines, while a second speaker chimed in with the short lines—'And so do I'. By this neat and simple stroke the unity of the poem was completely destroyed.

> This is the weather the cuckoo likes,
>   And so do I;
> When showers betumble the chestnut spikes,
>   And nestlings fly:
> And the little brown nightingale bills his best,
> And they sit outside at 'The Travellers' Rest',
> And maids come forth sprig-muslin drest,
> And citizens dream of the south and west,
>   And so do I.
>
> This is the weather the shepherd shuns,
>   And so do I;
> When beeches drip in browns and duns,
>   And thresh, and ply;

And hill-hid tides throb, throe on throe,
And meadow rivulets overflow,
And drops on gate-bars hang in a row,
And rooks in families homeward go,
    And so do I.

I am not sure that this is a poem which ought to be spoken chorally, but if it is, this was certainly not the way to do it.

Choral Speech may be described as a critical method of teaching poems, disguised as an active one. But more directly critical methods will often be appropriate, especially with older children. Many good poems will offer occasions for comprehension-work, often of a tough and difficult kind. In such cases the teacher's help will be needed on a considerable scale. Even when there is much commentary and criticism to be undertaken it will usually be best if the class has some sort of total impression of the poem, however imprecise, before it is 'pulled to pieces'. Some well-meaning people object to anything so sacrilegious as analysing a poem; but it never matters, provided the poem is put together again, and the total experience restored.

On the right occasion a teacher may give something like a continuous lecture on a particular poem. There is no need for him to feel that he must *always* 'get the answers out of the class'. It is possible for this ideal to become a fetish. A lecture or a short talk on Keats's *Ode to Autumn*, for instance, with a class of fourteen-year-olds would not be out of place, provided this is a poem the teacher admires and understands. He might begin by outlining the circumstances in which the poem was written, so that the class would feel something of the mood of tranquil resignation which gave rise to it. He might then read the poem, and ask the class to look at it for themselves. He could then point out how each of the three stanzas is concerned with a different way of experiencing autumn—the first, with the sight and taste and feel of its fruits; the second, with its drowsy heat, its warm and soporific smells, and the labours of the harvest; and the third, with the sounds of autumn. He could then show how in each stanza the diction is evocative of the mood, and the rhythm and movement of the lines expressive of a sad, yet contented, calm. Once the class had shown some appreciation of the poem, the teacher could go on to say something of the profound pathos of the final line, 'And gathering swallows twitter in the skies'. He could explain how the idea of the migration of birds was a recent scientific discovery, definitely established by Gilbert White only a few years before Keats was born. The application of the scientific fact to Keats' case was, of course, that the swallows were going south to the warm Mediterranean while Keats was obliged to spend the winter in the cold and damp of England, which he so much dreaded because it could only aggravate his tendency to consumption, the disease of which his brother Tom had died less than a year before. It was not until the following winter, a year after writing the *Ode to Autumn*, that Keats was able to go south, and then it was too late.

How much of this biographical commentary is appropriate must be left to the teacher as he considers the needs and interests of different classes. Obviously much of the incidental criticism of such a poem can be got from the class, so long as this does not involve matters of which they are not likely to have any knowledge. I do not suggest that a lecture or talk by the teacher is an ideal practice; it should be no more than an occasional one. There is much in the appreciation of a poem such as Keats's ode which can stimulate the pupils' powers of analysis and criticism. And much work of this kind will be appropriate in a full and varied poetry syllabus.

Further examples will be considered in later pages, but a few general remarks about critical appreciation will here be relevant. First, questions should be carefully prepared. The kind of random questioning which sometimes follows the reading of a poem because the teacher feels that something of the sort is required but does not quite know how to proceed —this is as good as useless. Provided the teacher comes to the class with a carefully prepared set of questions, valuable critical work can be done; and it does not much matter whether the questions are answered orally with the poem in front of the class, or with books shut, or as a written exercise. Sometimes the questions should be asked after a silent reading. In any case, however, the poem should never be treated simply as a basis for questions; the class should always end with a total experience of the poem, even if this is no more than a final re-reading by the teacher or by one of its members. Thirdly— and this is most important, and most often neglected—the questions should always be framed so as to direct attention back towards the poem, not outwards and away from it. Suppose, for example, the teacher is concerned with the scene of Shelley's sonnet *Ozymandias*.[1] The questions should be of this kind: Where do you think the scene of this poem might be? (Egypt, Libya, etc.) Why? What lines indicate that it is some-where with vast, featureless deserts? What is there in the poem which makes it unlikely that Northern Australia is intended? The questions should, on the other hand, not be of this kind: Where do you think the 'antique land' is? What do you know about Egypt? Describe the sphinx and the pyramids. What other words might have been used instead of 'antique'? What is a sculptor? Mention any sculptors whose names you know. What part of speech is 'mighty'? What does 'colossal' mean? All these questions lead the reader's attention away from the poem—towards history, or art, or grammar The poem is used merely as a basis for a lesson in general knowledge.

To the question, Should children learn poetry by heart? the ideal answer is, No, but they should *know* a good many poems by heart. To put it more fully, the old, mechanical 'repetition' lesson has little value—the lesson, that is, in which the teacher prescribes a poem which the class is expected to memorize before the next lesson, when they will be asked to write it out or recite it. On the other hand, a class which has been taught well and which has responded appreciatively to the poems it has studied will, almost automatically, know at least some of them by heart after a while. It will be a good thing to test this

[1] See p. 16.

knowledge either orally or by written work. After a thorough discussion of a short poem, and perhaps a choral performance, most of the class will know at least part of it by heart. When they have studied a poem, they can be asked, with books shut, to reconstruct the poem orally, with the necessary prompting from the teacher. Later, they may be told to refresh their memories of one poem out of a choice of several, and they will be given the opportunity for speaking the poem of their choice from memory. In Choral work it will inevitably happen that some of the poems studied will stay in the memory readily and can be performed all the better for being repeated without books. In short, memorization as a task, for its own sake, is pointless; memorization as a result of intelligent study or as an aid to performance, is valuable.

To sum up: poetry should be so taught that a poem is the centre of an active and pleasurable experience, not a text in black-and-white on the page of a book; the poetry lesson should be lively, and methods should be constantly varied. No poem should be studied for longer than interest can be maintained, and this period will be strictly limited in the case of the younger children. Juniors readily take to a new poem, and accept it eagerly as a new experience; but even a poem they enjoy immensely at first reading will bore them after a while. The point at which to stop studying any poem is when interest is at its height, not when it begins to flag. If this is observed, the class will ask for the same poem again, and a repetition of it may well be a suitable beginning for the next lesson. Young children should read and enjoy poetry uncritically; their interest cannot be expected to be profound, analytical or even sustained. Choral Speech is the ideal method of bridging the gap between critical and uncritical reading; it contains the germs of articulate aesthetic appreciation. Conscious literary appreciation can only be taught in the later stages of the school course—say at thirteen or fourteen years old. Even then it must not be laboured. The teacher's part in all poetry lessons will vary: he may read a new poem, he may talk about a poem or its writer, he may ask prepared questions and direct critical inquiries; or he may take a quite passive role, encouraging the class to choose its own poems, organize its own choral presentations, study poems silently. He may discover, with the Duke of Plaza Toro, that it is wisest to lead his regiment from behind. Above all, he must keep the lesson moving, avoid monotony, and preserve the elements of surprise, wonder, and enjoyment.

CHAPTER 3

INFANTS AND YOUNGER JUNIORS

(*5 to 8 Years Old*)

INFANTS and younger juniors are social animals. They like doing things in groups—not necessarily large groups: big classes should be divided into smaller groups which may compete with one another in speaking and acting poems. I hope this will not be taken as advocating a spirit of feverish emulation for a prize or for the teacher's approval. A spirit of moderate and friendly rivalry is healthy, especially between groups, not between individuals.

Infants are wrongly named. The word means 'the speechless ones'—a manifest absurdity. The teaching of poetry at this stage should be largely oral, though as soon as the children begin to read with any degree of confidence, they should be shown their favourite rhymes and poems in print. Obviously they cannot be expected to read a new poem from print for the first time when they are five or six years old; but by the time they are eight a reasonable fluency may be expected in reading simple, not over-long poems from books. At first, however, the emphasis must be on rhymes learnt from the teacher's lips and retained in the memory.

All children come to school with a knowledge of at least some nursery rhymes learnt on, or at, their mother's knee. Most children actively enjoy and treasure the rhymes they know, and it is on this firm, though perhaps not deep, foundation that further progress can be built. The qualities which endear nursery rhymes to young children are these: vigorous and well-marked rhythm; concrete and homely language, sensuously realizable—sight, hearing, touch, taste and even smell are called into play; simple events or situations devoid of sentimentality, not necessarily complete but having at any rate the appearance of finality. There is no room in a good nursery rhyme, or in a child's mind, for whimsicality, vague atmospherics, or humanitarian sentiment—except of the simplest and most obvious kind. Children recognize the cruelty of Johnny Green in dropping the kitten down the well, but their feelings are only outraged theoretically; just as they can contemplate with complete equanimity the equally theoretical episode of the Farmers' Wife and the Three Blind Mice; this is a merry song, not because it is an account of cruelty under the influence of panic fear, but because it is an exploration into language and rhyme, rhythm and movement. An adult may justifiably find the rhyme unacceptable, provided he realizes that it is beyond a child's powers to be morally outraged.

The nursery rhyme world, in which nearly all children dwell with delight and security, as well as innocence, is at least half imaginary: it is self-sufficient, existing somewhere between reality and nonsense, true to its own laws, and having as its purpose the celebration of language. Delight in words is the peculiar quality of this world. A satisfactory rhyme is as magical a possession to a child as any ball, rattle or toy animal. We cannot linger in the nursery rhyme world, for it is prior to the world of the class room. I do not mean that nursery rhymes should be excluded from the class room; but rather, that we have to consider how to extend the child's experience beyond the familiar rhymes, whose enjoyment was essentially a transaction between the child and his mother; we have to consider what other poems can continue this early experience of language and enlarge it to apply to a group.

I have been criticized for including the words of folk-songs in collections of poems for schools. I am unrepentant. The divorce which has occurred in recent centuries between poetry and music obscures the fact that there was once a natural and apparently indissoluble marriage between them. The rhythm of poetry is partly a vestigial survival from its origins in the song and the dance. That children should *sing* rather than speak the words of folk-songs I do not deny; but this is not done in all schools. That the poetry lesson and the music lesson are separated from each other has often seemed to me a pity. Where they are taken by the same teacher, or where collaboration exists between the teachers of the two subjects, much can be done to re-unite them. Even so, many folk-songs do not have tunes which recommend themselves to young singers. The tunes of others are lost. For instance, I do not know of a tune to *John Cook's Mare*.

> John Cook he had a little grey mare;
>   *Hee, haw, hum!*
> Her back stood up, and her bones they were bare;
>   *Hee, haw, hum!*
>
> John Cook was riding up Shooter's Bank;
>   *Hee, haw, hum!*
> And there his nag did kick and prank . . .
>
> John Cook was riding up Shooter's Hill . . .
> His mare fell down and she made her will . . .
>
> The saddle and bridle are laid on the shelf . . .
> If you want any more you may sing it yourself! . . .

This is an excellent poem to teach infants and young juniors. The class should first be told to say in unison the refrain-line *Hee, haw, hum!* Once they can do this with vigour and confidence, the teacher should tell the story of John Cook and his mare line by line, asking the children to say the refrain after each line in a suitable tone. Line 1 will be introductory; line 2, spoken more lugubriously, expresses the poor condition of the horse; line 3 will suggest a vigorous, upward movement; line 4 will indicate heightened excitement; line 5 is the climax of the poem, and line 6 the disastrous anticlimax. Lines 7 and 8 dismiss the episode in a light-hearted and matter-of-fact manner.

Eight times the class is expected to say the refrain in variously expressive tones of voice. This is a simple exercise in vocal expressiveness, and one which all children enjoy. They will have no difficulty in memorizing the poem, after which different groups may take it in turns to speak the story-lines and the refrain.

A poem which may be spoken in unison by a group or by the whole class is Walter de la Mare's *Five Eyes*, which has the best of the nursery rhyme qualities and is at the same time a good example of de la Mare's highly personal idiom.

> In Hans' old Mill his three black cats
> Watch the bins for the thieving rats.
> Whisker and claw, they crouch in the night,
> Their five eyes smouldering green and bright;
> Squeaks from the flour sacks, squeaks from where
> The cold wind stirs on the empty stair,
> Squeaking and scampering everywhere.
> Then down they pounce, now in, now out,
> At whisking tail and sniffing snout;
> While lean old Hans he snores away
> Till peep of light at break of day;
> Then up he climbs to his creaking mill,
> Out come his cats all grey with meal—
> Jekkel, and Jessup, and one-eyed Jill.

This is a poem which lends itself to two extremes of bad speaking: its neatness of phrase and musical clarity invite over-precision; the names of the cats, as well as phrases such as 'whisker and claw', should indeed be spoken crisply, but excessive crispness takes away from the naturalness of the performance and recalls the old-fashioned 'elocution' lesson.

On the other hand, any reading of *Five Eyes*, particularly a unison group reading, may become mechanical and dead, because of the strongly marked rhythm. The question of what to do about 'sing-song' is always an urgent one, and never more so than at the junior stage.

Any good reading of poetry must proceed, as it were, from

the *inside*—that is, from a sensuous and, to whatever extent necessary, intellectual appreciation of the poem. If it is on the one hand merely mechanical, or, on the other hand, imposed from outside, through some preconceived idea of what constitutes the proper way to read a poem, no matter what poem, it will be a wrong reading, because a lifeless one. I do not know which is worse—the monotonous sing-song of a class which is not thinking about what it is saying, because it cannot understand it or is bored, or the over-refined, artificial rendering of a poem by a pupil who has had private elocution lessons, and knows the kind of voice, tone and tricks to adopt when reading poetry aloud. The rule is that the mind of the speaker must be focused on the meaning of the poem, not on the manner of reading. He must aim at expressing his understanding and appreciation of the poem through the medium of his voice. A simple instance will show what I mean.

I once went into a class of infants to find them reciting in unison the nursery rhyme of *Ladybird, Ladybird*. The recitation was mechanical and meaningless; it had become a mere ritual chant. Now it is possible to maintain that this rhyme has little more meaning than, say, 'Eeny meeny miny mo', but I think otherwise, and so, I believe, did the student in charge of the class, who seemed to share my dissatisfaction with the recitation without knowing just what to do about it. There is, after ell, an inoffensive and charming miniature creature which we call a ladybird, and which, to judge from its name, was once credited with some divine significance or associations. But it occurred to me that not all the class were quite clear as to what the insect looked like. So I asked for a show of hands as to who did not know what a ladybird was. A number did not know. One of the others instructed them. Next I suggested that they should speak the poem as if they were really addressing a living creature; and to make this easier, I told them each to raise his right forefinger and picture a ladybird sitting on top. I then told them to say the poem again, not bothering whether or not they were all keeping together, but being sure to speak as if they were warning their particular insect of its danger. The difference in the tone and liveliness of the recitation far exceeded anything I had expected. It was this experiment which taught me the importance of the rule that good reading comes as a result of thinking intensely about what is being read, realizing it with the senses and not simply the intellect. The moment this intensity is relaxed, the reading becomes mechanical; possibly the class is bored and needs a change. Many teachers, especially the inexperienced, go on too long with the same poem.

I do not propose to say a great deal about speech training as such, partly because I am not an expert, and partly because the whole subject needs special treatment. One does not, however, need to be an expert to realize that constant insistence on brightness and vigour of tone and attack are necessary; that lazy and slovenly articulation, due nearly always to slackness in opening the mouth wide enough, makes pleasing speech impossible; and that some sort of constant practice is useful and, in most schools, essential. Teachers who are alarmed at the idea of encroaching on what they may consider a specialist's territory will be surprised at the effect of a few minutes' regular work on speech-rhymes before the real lesson begins. There are several excellent collections of these rhymes,[1] which have the great merit that, not pretending to be poetry, they can be used as practice material without scruple. In fact, the best of them are worthy to take their place with the traditional nursery rhymes, and there is no need whatever for the use of sheer rubbish for this purpose. They are, too, composed specially to emphasize particular speech situations. An unpleasant throaty tone, for example, is caused by speaking too far back; and a forward tone, as it is called, which is essential for clarity of diction, is assisted by practising the nasal sounds 'm', 'n' and 'ng'. Accordingly the best collections of speech-rhymes contain examples in which these sounds predominate.

[1] Clive Sansom: *Speech Rhymes* (Black). Mona Swann: *Trippingly on the Tongue* (Macmillan).

A most effective rhyme invented by Mr Clive Sansom for practice in nasal resonance and sustained tone runs as follows:

LIGHTSHIPS[1]

All night long when the wind is high,
   NnnnnnNnnnnnNnnnnn,
The lightships moan and moan to the sky,
   NnnnnnNnnnnnNnnnnn.

Their foghorns whine when the mist runs free,
   NnnnnnNnnnnnNnnnnn,
Warning the men on the ships at sea,
   NnnnnnNnnnnnNnnnnn.

Here the refrain line is an imitation of the sound of a foghorn; it is spoken, or hummed, in one breath and on one note, but with a triple accentuation, indicated by the capital N's.

Another of Mr Sansom's rhymes, designed for agility in tongue movement, is called

CLOCKS AND WATCHES[1]

Our great
Steeple clock
Goes TICK—TOCK,
TICK—TOCK;

Our small
Mantel clock
Goes TICK-TACK, TICK-TACK,
TICK-TACK, TICK-TACK;

Our little
Pocket watch
Goes Tick-a-tacker, tick-a-tacker,
Tick-a-tacker, tick.

[1] Clive Sansom: *Speech Rhymes*, Book II (Black).

Once the class can say the rhyme correctly as a whole, they may be divided into three equal groups, which can speak the three verses simultaneously, each occupying exactly the same space of time. The TICK-TACKS of verse 2 are spoken exactly twice as fast, and the Tick-a-tackers of verse 3 four times as fast, as the TICK-TOCKS of verse 1.

Both of these rhymes are thoroughly enjoyed by children, and with material like this speech training becomes a delightful and satisfying game.

Another rhyme which can scarcely be called a poem, but which encourages expressive reading, is Mr Robert Graves's

A COUGH

> I have a little cough, sir,
> In my little chest, sir,
> Every time I cough, sir,
> It leaves a little pain, sir,
> Ahem! ahem! ahem! ahem!
> There it is again, sir.

A difficulty which often arises once boys get beyond the infant stage is that they begin to regard such things as fairies as unmanly and worthy only of the attention of their sisters. But it is a pity that such a prejudice should debar them from the enjoyment of a poem like William Allingham's *The Fairies*.

> Up the airy mountain,
>   Down the rushy glen,
> We daren't go a-hunting
>   For fear of little men.

It should be noticed that the word 'fairies' occurs only in the title and not in the poem. It might be explained that the writer was an Irishman, and that in Ireland, at least until recently, most country folk believed in 'the little men' or the 'wee folk', as they were called.

A most suitable kind of poem for class study with younger juniors is *The Fox*.[1] This is the folk-song beginning

> The fox went out one winter night,

and having after each verse a refrain which takes up the last word, and then the last two lines, of the verse. There is nothing in the poem which calls for explanation; and here it may be said in parenthesis that with younger juniors verbal explanations should be kept to a minimum, if not avoided altogether. A good choice of verse will automatically extend the range of their vocabulary, though this is not an important function of poetry at this stage. The extension of vocabulary will come mainly through prose texts and readers. The magic of poetry should not be dulled by overmuch explanation. Nobody now uses the word 'crown' for the top of the head in ordinary speech, yet no infant listening to, or repeating, *Jack and Jill* wants to be told exactly what it was Jack broke.

As has been said before, and will be insisted on continually, every poem is different from every other poem. The best method of reading it in class will suggest itself after a study of its unique quality. A reader with sufficient vocal and dramatic flexibility—a teacher, perhaps, but certainly not a child of seven or eight—can make an exciting performance of *The Fox* as a solo speaker, with the class coming in at the refrain. But a more enjoyable method is one in which a number of groups and individuals can participate.

> The fox went out one winter night,
> And prayed the moon to give him light,
> For he'd many a mile to go that night,
>   Before he reached his den, oh!
> *Chorus.* Den, oh! Den, oh!
>   For he'd many a mile to go that night,
>   He'd many a mile to go that night,
>   Before he reached his den, oh!

---

[1] See pp. 31–32. If the class cannot sing this song, let them enjoy it as performed on a gramophone record by Burl Ives.

At last he came to a farmer's yard,
Where the ducks and geese were all afear'd.
'The best of you all shall grease my beard,
   Before I leave the town, oh!'
Chorus. Town, oh! Town, oh!
   'The best of you all . . .'

He took the grey goose by the neck,
He laid a duck across his back,
And heeded not their quack! quack! quack!
   The legs all dangling down, oh!
Chorus. Down, oh! Down, oh!
   And heeded not their . . .

Then Old Mother Slipper-Slopper jumped out of bed
And out of the window she popped her head,
Crying, 'Oh! John, John! the grey goose is dead,
   And the fox is over the down, oh!'
Chorus. Down, oh! Down, oh!
   Crying, 'Oh! John, John! . . .'

Then John got up to the top of the hill,
And blew his horn both loud and shrill,
'Blow on,' said Reynard, 'your music still,
   Whilst I trot home to my den, oh!'
Chorus. Den, oh! Den, oh!
   'Blow on,' said Reynard . . .

At last he came to his cosy den,
Where sat his young ones nine or ten.
Quoth they, 'Daddy, you must go there again,
   For sure 'tis a lucky town, oh!'
Chorus. Town, oh! Town, oh!
   Quoth they, 'Daddy . . .'

The fox and his wife without any strife,
They cut up the goose without fork or knife,
And said 'twas the best they had ate in their life,
   And the young ones picked the bones, oh!

Chorus. Bones, oh! Bones, oh!
    And said 'twas the best . . .

Each of the seven verses relates part of the story, though five of
them also contain words or lines in direct speech. The appropriate method, therefore, is to have the narration read either by
the teacher, or by a single member of the class, or by a small
group. The whole class will read the refrain after each verse.
In verse 2 a reader (or small group) will be required for
Reynard, the fox; in verse 3 the cry of 'Quack, quack, quack'
may be given to a small group; in verse 4 Mother Slipper-
Slopper speaks in her own person; in verse 5 Reynard speaks
again; and in verse 6 a group of fox-cubs is heard. The two
outer verses (1 and 7) are spoken entirely by the narrator.

The mere fact of allotting 'parts' in the performance of a
poem of this kind is nearly sufficient to ensure lively and
dramatic eading. The only thing that may perhaps dull the
response of children to this sort of work is an excess of choral
speaking, a habitual choice of poems requiring the same sort of
treatment.

Nevertheless, there is no question but that active methods
of reading poems are the most suitable for younger juniors. If
they do not happen to sing *Soldier, Soldier*, it makes an excellent choice for dramatized speaking.

> 'Soldier, soldier, won't you marry me,
>   With your musket, fife and drum?'
> 'Oh, no, sweet maid, I cannot marry you,
>   For I have no hat to put on.'
>
> So up she went to her grandfather's chest,
>   And she got him a hat of the very, very best,
>   And the soldier put it on!
>
> 'Soldier, soldier, won't you marry me
>   With your musket, fife and drum?'
> 'Oh no, sweet maid, I cannot marry you,
>   For I have no coat to put on.'

So up she went to her grandfather's chest,
And she got him a coat of the very, very best,
    And the soldier put it on!

'Soldier, soldier, won't you marry me,
    With your musket, fife and drum?'
'Oh no, sweet maid, I cannot marry you,
    For I have no boots to put on.'

So up she went to her grandfather's chest,
And she got him a pair of the very, very best,
    And the soldier put them on!

'Soldier, soldier, won't you marry me,
    With your musket, fife and drum?'
'Oh no, sweet maid, I cannot marry you,
    For I have a wife of my own!'

One group of children can say the words of the girl, and another those of the soldier, while a third group (or possibly the
whole class) can say the narrative lines. While the narration is
in progress the girl group and the soldier group can act the lines
in mime.

There is no space to deal in detail with the subject of mime,
but with the age-group in question it should always be kept in
the teacher's mind as a possibility for use with the right kind of
poem. One of the most enjoyable lessons I ever took part in
was an attempt to mime the poem about King Arthur and the
bag pudding.

There was not much time left, so I read the poem first, asking
the class (a large class of bright seven-year-olds) to think of
suitable actions to represent the King, the Queen, the nobles
who ate the pudding, and the pudding itself. They were able
to suggest the contrast between the King's alleged piety and his
actual knavery, first by joining their hands in prayer and then by
a series of stealthy, sidelong glances; my own vocal expression
emphasized the contrast. A rounded gesture of both hands
indicated the pudding, and a thumbs-up sign hinted at the

lumps of fat. In the next verse a pompous feast was easily and simply suggested, and at the end came the most delightful touch of all: it came entirely spontaneously from several of the girls in the class and instantly spread to everyone else. Not only was it something I would never have had the imagination to invent, but it showed how readily these seven-year-olds entered into the spirit of mime and grasped its purpose. As soon as I said the word 'fried', I noticed that the girls' right hands went out in front of them in the gesture of one holding a pan over a flame, and from their mouths came the most appetizing sound of sizzling. The effect was quite unrehearsed. Afterwards, having rapidly learnt the three verses by heart, the whole class spoke the poem with relish and performed the agreed actions as they did so.

One way to ensure close and intelligent attention is to choose a suitable narrative poem, generally rather longer than *King Arthur*, and invite the class to comment silently by means of mime.

These are only a few of the ways in which poetry can be taught to the younger juniors. It will have been noticed that they are all non-critical: obviously at this stage conscious criticism is out of place; yet even when the children are listening, they need by no means be inactive. The essence of all poetry teaching at present is that it should be active, oral, and where possible dramatic. Where it is possible to arrange this, the lessons should not be longer than twenty minutes, or half an hour at most. With infants especially, a poetry lesson may be fitted into the timetable at the moment when the class is most ready for it, and need not be of a set length. The choice of poems should be varied, and while favourite poems may be repeated in successive lessons almost indefinitely, no one poem should occupy the attention of the class for long at a time. Each lesson should begin with one or two speech rhymes, taking perhaps five minutes; next, a new poem should be introduced; or, if the teacher considers it more suitable, one studied previously may be repeated. On the whole, it is better to introduce new material to start with, and then return to something familiar. In this way, a fair stock of poems is stored in the children's minds, and soon they will know most of them by heart. There is no reason why some of their favourites should not be copied down, though only such things as speech rhymes should be used as writing practice.

If regular practice is given, standards of speech and oral interpretation will improve with certainty and even with speed. The qualities to be aimed at are, in this order: (1) boldness, energy, vigour; (2) clarity, neatness of phrase; (3) agreeable tone, correctness of vowel pronunciation. Most of the faults of speech that children come to school with, or pick up like an infection from the worst offenders, are due to laziness in breathing or in lip-movements. This is remedied more by regular practice than by specific theoretical instruction. The teacher should not expect rapid progress in the direction of 'standard' pronunciation, especially in a district where bad habits prevail. He must remember that speech-training is a process which goes on throughout a child's school life. The main thing at this stage is that the poetry should be enjoyed for its own sake. It may be thought that in this chapter the poems I have discussed are too light and trivial in character; but they are all poems or rhymes of the right kind—vigorous, concrete, unsentimental ; there is nothing solemn or didactic, though more serious poems, such as Psalms or short passages from the Bible, also have their place. The great thing is that the poetry lesson should be lively and varied, so that the associations which the children form round the idea of poetry are pleasurable; a poem is something to be looked forward to as a fresh experience, worked at, retained in the memory. Few children mind hard work, but none relish drudgery.

A final word about the kind of poems to avoid at this stage. Most whimsy and sentimentality is due to false notions about child nature on the part of misguided adults. Archness, coyness, mere prettiness should be avoided. Children, especially girls, may be encouraged easily enough to enjoy mediocre ditties about nature, pets and fairies; but the result of this sort of thing is an early disgust with all poetry on the part of boys, and the ultimate turning away from all poetry by both girls and boys, as being childish and unreal. Poems which are ultimately destructive of poetic taste are found in most junior school poetry books. The sort I have in mind can best be typified by an imitation—exaggerated perhaps, but recognizable.

A THOUGHT

I wish I were a bumble bee
  So merry, blithe and gay,
To buzz and hum from flower to flower
  All on a summer's day.

I wish I were a butterfly
  Upon a buttercup.
I'd flutter down the woodland paths
  And then I'd flutter up.

I wish I were—but then, oh dear!
  A sudden thought strikes me:
For if I were a butterfly,
  I could not be a bee.

I'd love to be a bumble bee
  All summer time, and so
I'm glad I'm not a butterfly
  To flutter to and fro.

CHAPTER 4

JUNIORS

(8 to 11 Years Old)

IN the last three years of the primary school course the main work in the teaching of poetry will be to extend the range of the children's appreciation, to increase their powers of interpretation through speech, to initiate the rudiments of a critical or analytical attitude, and to encourage creative work.

The speech-rhymes mentioned in the previous chapter should be continued, with perhaps more exacting standards of proficiency. The interpretation of poems through choral verse should continue to be a major activity, and so long as the children have been encouraged in this form of group work, it can do no harm to begin some attempt at solo performance. 'Recitation', in the sense of a personal exhibition or a memory-test, is not what is wanted; but if a group can perform a poem in unison, there is no harm in informal solo performance, provided this is not carried on in a competitive spirit. Let a solo performance rather be something that is done for the enjoyment of the others. A child might come out in front of the class and read, or speak from memory, Lewis Carroll's marvellously suggestive lines entitled *Jabberwocky*. This is a fine opportunity for expressiveness in excess, as it were, of what is being expressed. It is a unique piece of mock terror and should be taken with deadly seriousness. It should be the aim of the speaker to conjure up a scene of vague, but blood-chilling frightfulness. Most children, encouraged to 'let themselves go', revel in the sheer sound of the words, not indeed devoid of meaning but charged with a meaning deeper and more significant than that of everyday language. *Jabberwocky* is, on its own level, pure poetry.

The appreciation of poetry, though I shall suggest some ways in which it may be made somewhat critical, will in the main still take the form of active enjoyment. Indeed, there is a place also for passive enjoyment—a 'lesson' in which the class sits back in an attitude of relaxation and listens while the teacher reads to them may be a valuable change from the usual 'active' lesson. For such a reading he should choose a longer poem than is usually read by the class, perhaps a ballad or other narrative poem. If the poem chosen, read as expressively as possible, does not ensure close attention, it is not well chosen; there should be no need to test attention by asking questions about the meaning and content of the poem. If children enjoy a good poem, that in itself is educative. Not that questions are always to be deprecated; on the contrary, I shall give examples of how appreciation can be heightened by suitable questioning.

Most children of about eight enjoy, for instance, Keats's rhyme *A Naughty Boy*. Let them read, learn and repeat the rhyme with as much liveliness and expression as possible. The reading should not, however, be so laboured as to lose the quality of spontaneity: it was an almost extempore rhyme composed for the amusement of Keats's young sister.

There was a naughty boy,
    And a naughty boy was he,
He ran away to Scotland,
    The people there to see—
    Then he found
    That the ground
    Was as hard,
    That a yard
    Was as long,
    That a song
    Was as merry,
    That a cherry

Was as red,
That lead
Was as weighty,
That fourscore
Was as eighty,
That a door
Was as wooden
As in England—
So he stood in his shoes
And he wondered,
He wondered,
He stood in his shoes
And he wondered.

One of the attractions of Keats's poetry is its immediate appeal to the senses; and it need hardly be insisted on that it is one of the functions of poetry, especially at the junior stage, to nourish and stimulate a sharp sensuous awareness of the natural world. Let the children name the five senses, and then search through *A Naughty Boy* for lines which appeal to each of them. They will discover that there is nothing which appeals to the nose, but plenty that appeals to the other senses. At a slightly later age children will appreciate Keats's *Meg Merrilies* for the same sensuous qualities—and once they know that 'woodbine' is honeysuckle, they will see that even the sense of smell has been catered for.

Some poetry books intended for children are arranged so that poems on similar subjects come together: there may be, for example, a group of poems about animals, followed by a group on spring or winter, and another on ships and the sea. This is a mistake. Undoubtedly it is a convenient arrangement for the teacher who supposes it is natural to read two or three poems on the same subject in one lesson. But it fosters the idea that the main thing about a poem is its subject. Children need variety and contrast, not sameness. An equally, perhaps more, logical arrangement would be to group poems with the same metre together. But there is no need for any such arbitrary grouping.

Every poem exists in its own right and for its own reasons. It is true that a poetry lesson is sometimes given a spurious unity by being concerned with three poems about, say, domestic animals; and this is harmless enough so long as it is not made the regular thing. Three poems which might well be read in succession are Walter de la Mare's *Sooeep* and *The Old Tailor*, and the anonymous rhyme *The Jolly Miller*.

'SOOEEP'

Black as a chimney is his face,
 And ivory white his teeth,
And in his brass-bound cart he rides,
 The chestnut blooms beneath.

'Sooeep, Sooeep!' he cries, and brightly peers
 This way and that, to see
With his two light-blue shining eyes
 What custom there may be.

And once inside the house, he'll squat,
 And drive his rods on high,
Till twirls his sudden sooty brush
 Against the morning sky.

Then 'mid his bulging bags of soot,
 With half the world asleep,
His small cart wheels him off again,
 Still hoarsely bawling, 'Sooeep!'

THE OLD TAILOR

There was once an old Tailor of Hickery Mo,
Too tired at evening to sew, to sew:
He put by his needle, he snapped his thread,
And, cross-legged, sang to his fiddle instead.
His candle bobbed at each note that came
And spat out a spark from the midst of its flame:

His catgut strings they yelped and yawled,
The wilder their scrapings the louder he bawled;
The grease strickled over at every beat,
Welled down to the stick in a winding-sheet—
Till up sprang puss from the fire, with a *WOW*!
'A *fine* kakkamangul you're making now!'

THE JOLLY MILLER

There was a jolly miller once
   Lived on the River Dee.
He worked so hard from morn till night,
   No lark so blithe as he.

And this the burden of his song
   For ever used to be,
'I care for nobody, no, not I,
   If nobody cares for me.'

In the first of these the children might be asked to point out
lines which help them to *see* the sweep and his cart; in the
second they could be asked to find words expressive of strange
sounds; in reading *The Jolly Miller* they might be asked whether
they find it easier or harder to picture the miller than the sweep
and the tailor—and why.

This group of poems might be used as the occasion for
original work; the children could be asked to make a drawing
of one of the three characters. This will help them to visualize
what they are reading. It must not be forgotten that reading
a poem may be a purely intellectual experience; but this is not
the right kind of experience for juniors. They must be made to
feel it as an experience of sound and colour, rhythm and
texture. A poem, certainly, is made of words; but if it is
realized simply as words, it will not come alive.

A marvellously vivid and concrete poem is Shakespeare's
When icicles hang by the wall which is a series of brilliant
miniatures of country life in winter. It is, I think, appropriate
to the form of this poem to speak this in the following way:

give each of the first six lines of each verse to a separate speaker (or small group), with a larger group (or the whole class) saying the refrain lines at the end of each verse. So the first speaker has 'When icicles hang by the wall', the second 'And Dick the shepherd blows his nail', the third 'When Tom bears logs into the hall'—and so on. If each speaker not only says his line in such a way as to make its meaning clearly visible (or audible in some cases), but also listens attentively to the other lines (speaking them, as it were, silently), not only will the force of each separate picture be emphasized, but the unity of the poem need not be lost through a disjointed reading. I do not suggest that this would necessarily make an impressive 'performance' for outsiders to listen to; but it would bring home to the children taking part the essential, unique form of the poem—its unity in diversity. Every line requires its particular mood and emphasis—the word 'icicles' must be made to _sound_ cold, and we must be able to _see_ the birds 'brooding in the snow'.

A poem similarly composed of a succession of separate yet related pictures is Hardy's *Weathers*; but here there is a contrast in mood between the two verses, not a continuation of the same mood, as in Shakespeare's poem. The great difference, however, between the two poems is that Shakespeare's is objective—the writer does not come into it at all—while Hardy's is personal. I think, therefore, that if the poem is split up, its unity may be lost: it would be better to read it in unison, aiming at the maximum expressiveness of the two contrasting moods by the whole group. In speaking *Weathers* nothing should be done which suggests that it is not *one* person speaking throughout; this does not hold good for *When icicles hang by the wall*.

However much discussion, analysis and questioning is carried on, nothing should be done to destroy the sense of mystery and wonder possessed by young children, but easily destroyed or dulled by too much factual learning. It is one of the main functions of poetry at this stage to nourish and stimulate the sense of wonder, the sense of the inexhaustible magic of the world.

Old Shellover by Walter de la Mare is a perfect example of how a poet can transmute an ordinary occurrence of nature into a magical experience.

> 'Come!' said Old Shellover.
> 'What?' says Creep.
> The horny old Gardener's fast asleep;
> The fat cock Thrush
> To his nest has gone,
> And the dew shines bright
> In the rising Moon;
> Old Sally Worm from her hole doth peep;
> 'Come!' said Old Shellover.
> 'Ay!' said Creep.

The teacher might begin by reading it in a voice which conveys something of the hushed, expectant atmosphere of a moonlight night in summer. Then he could ask the class to say what the two speakers, Shellover and Creep, are. The former is a snail, though I once had to explain to a child of eight why her answer of 'tortoise', though ingenious, could not be right. Creep must be a slug, since 'Old Sally Worm' is specifically mentioned. Then the class can be encouraged to think a little about the poem by being asked a few questions like: 'What adjective is used to describe the gardener? Why is "horny" a good word? (Because it suggests that he is toughened by the weather, and that he is well able to crush offending snails and slugs.) Apart from "bright", which is really only part of the verb "shines", and "old", which is scarcely descriptive at all, there is only one other descriptive word. What is it? ("Fat.") Why is it a good word to apply to the cock thrush? (It suggests that he is greedy, and over-fond of slugs and snails.)' In this way the children can be made to understand that atmosphere can be achieved through economy of statement, and that one or two well-chosen adjectives are better than a whole dictionary-full. More than this, they can be made to feel something of the interest to be found in the lives of even the most despised of creatures.

An equally effective approach might be the indirect one: 'Which of you have seen a garden on a warm moonlight night in summer?' The children reconstruct the atmosphere of silence, cool dew, and the appearance of small, defenceless creatures that dare come out only at night. Then, when expectation has been aroused, they are told that Walter de la Mare wrote a poem about just this atmosphere—and here it is. The important thing is that they should realize, perhaps only dimly, that everything in nature has a life of its own, however humble and secret, and that there is mystery in it, and that out of this mystery poetry can be made. When a few questions have been asked on the lines suggested, the poem should be put together again—that is, presented as a whole; and in this case, since it is such a brief one, this can best be done by asking the class to repeat the poem without books. They will not find this difficult, even though they have studied it for no more than ten minutes.

Another poem—for somewhat older juniors—which in my experience is best approached indirectly is *Blow, blow, thou winter wind*. 'What does "ingratitude" mean? Which of you has ever felt ill-used? You've done something to please somebody and they haven't noticed or shown any appreciation. Well, how do you let off your feelings of annoyance? How do you express this sense of not being appreciated?' Some such questions direct the children's minds to the idea of ingratitude, on which the poem is based. The teacher continues: 'This is how one of the people in a play by Shakespeare expressed the feeling of being ill-used.

> Blow, blow, thou winter wind,
> Thou art not so unkind
> As man's ingratitude . . .

I do not think this poem should be paraphrased. It is enough if the class appreciates the sound of the words and accepts the poem as an expression of strong emotion. If they ask the meaning of 'warp', 'benefits' or 'feigning', well and good. Essentially, however, this is a poem of which children need comprehend only the general sense; a sufficient test of their response will be to ask them which lines they can recall most readily after reading the poem two or three times. A lively and intelligent class may well follow the poem by a discussion of the idea that 'Most friendship is feigning, most loving mere folly'. So much the better; but this can hardly be expected of the average class of ten-year-olds.

Nature and human nature are the perennial themes of poetry. So also is the supernatural world, the world of pure fantasy. There is real poetry in the nonsense verse of Edward Lear, and children of seven or eight can be excited and spell-bound by 'the lands where the Jumblies live' and the still more wonderful voyage undertaken by these rash adventurers.

> And all night long they sailed away;
>   And when the sun went down,
> They whistled and warbled a moony song
> To the echoing sound of a coppery gong,
>   In the shade of the mountains brown.
> 'O Timballo! How happy we are,
> When we live in a sieve and a crockery-jar,
> And all night long in the moonlight pale,
> We sail away with a pea-green sail,
>   In the shade of the mountains brown!'
>   *Far and few, far and few,*
>   *Are the lands where the Jumblies live;*
>   *Their heads are green, and their hands are blue,*
>   *And they went to sea in a sieve.*

If a class is excited by this poem, it will do no harm to ask them to name as many as possible of the things brought back by the Jumblies; to recall the words of those who advised them not to go to sea in a sieve—first of all before the voyage and then afterwards; to mention some of the imaginary places visited by the Jumblies. But such questioning should not be too detailed or too insistent. There should be no lesson in the geography of so insubstantial a world. Far better that children should be encouraged to feel its magic through the sound of the words, the wonderful incantation of the chorus; and they can do this by speaking the poem out loud, with different groups of speakers for the narration, the Jumblies, the Jumblies' friends, and the chorus.

There is much nonsense that is very near to poetry and much poetry that is near to nonsense; that the two sometimes overlap is due to the irrational element in poetry; poetry is *not* prose thoughts expressed in verse, though we often treat it as if it were. Poems are often written in defiance of reason. So much of what children learn at school—Mathematics, Science, Grammar—is rational that we cannot afford to neglect whatever offers an escape from reason, an excursion out of the realm of necessity into that of improbability and the imagination.

> The lunatic, the lover and the poet
> Are of imagination all compact.

Here is a piece of apparent lunacy which any ingenious child will enjoy when he sees the trick of it.

> I saw a peacock with a fiery tail
> I saw a blazing comet drop down hail
> I saw a cloud wrapped with ivy round
> I saw an oak creep on along the ground
> I saw a serpent swallow up a whale
> I saw the sea brim-full of ale
> I saw a Venice glass five fathom deep
> I saw a well full of men's tears that weep
> I saw red eyes all of a flaming fire
> I saw a house bigger than the moon and higher
> I saw the sun at twelve o'clock at night
> I saw the man that saw this wondrous sight.

It is simply a matter of punctuation. Put a full-stop after 'I saw a peacock', read the next sentence as 'With a fiery tail I saw a blazing comet', continue in this way until the end of the poem, and the conundrum is explained. Clearly the possibilities here are inexhaustible, and an intelligent class with some practice in verse-writing might make up some lines of their own in imitation.

This brings us to the consideration of original work. In principle it is right that children should approach all artistic study from the standpoint of the creative worker. That the vast majority will not, in fact, grow up to become poets, artists, and musicians is beside the point: children draw pictures not in order to become artists but in order to learn to see; they write crude and probably unmusical tunes in order to train their ears; they write poems in order to know how to express their feelings in words—in order to realize as much as possible of their experience articulately. Whenever occasion happens, children should be encouraged to make their own poems. The class room does not offer the best atmosphere for this, but the teacher must use whatever opportunities he can. Apart from free verse composition on whatever subjects appeal to the class, here are some practical suggestions for creative work based on poetry.

First, the illustration of poems—or rather, the making of drawings and paintings inspired by poems. Obviously this can be carried too far. A drawing of a slug or a snail after reading *Old Shellover* would be of very little use; but making a drawing can, given the right material, assist the full comprehension and realization of a poem. To make a drawing inspired by something in the opening lines of Coleridge's *Christabel* or de la Mare's *Nicholas Nye* is one way of stimulating the pictorial sense and demands a more than usually careful and responsive reading of the poem.

Such illustrations might be made part of an anthology which every child keeps for himself in an exercise-book reserved for the purpose. The recording of a favourite poem will be a special occasion demanding 'best handwriting' and unusual neatness.

Exercises in verse composition on the model of poems read in class are also valuable. Such things give help to the non-literary child, especially in allowing him to feel that he can make something of his own in words, however difficult a medium he finds them. The child with a gift for words will or course readily compose verses of his own without artificial stimulation; but we are here considering the average child.

Some children succeed in achieving passable limericks; the very rigidity of the form is a help. It is often found, however, that the rather unusual limerick rhythm (anapaestic rather than the more usual iambic) does not come easily, so that not much should be expected in this form.

The Three Jovial Welshmen provides a useful framework for some simple work in imaginative writing. After the introductory verse, the pattern of the poem is as follows:

> All the day they hunted,
>   And nothing could they find
> But a *ship a-sailing*,
>   *A-sailing with the wind.*
>
> One said it was a *ship*;
>   The other he said nay;
> The third said it was *a house*
>   *With the chimney blown away.*

All that is necessary, in order to provide additional verses for this poem, is to supply new objects and words in place of those in italics. In order to make rhyming easier, the word 'find' at the end of line 2 can be replaced by 'see' or 'hear', and 'nay' at the end of line 6 can be replaced by 'no' or some other appropriate word.

A variation of this is to compose some verses using the refrain of a folk-song, such as *The Farmer's Daughters*.

> A farmer he lived in the west country,
>   *With a hey down, bow down!*
> A farmer he lived in the west country,
> And he had daughters, one, two, and three,
>   *Singing I will be true to my love*
>   *If my love will be true to me.*

On examination this pleasingly rhythmical verse is found to contain only two basic lines:

> A farmer he lived in the west country,
> And he had daughters, one, two, and three.

A class can write a few simple couplets of their own and arrange them in the same form as *The Farmer's Daughters*. The teacher may have to supply an opening verse. Almost anything will do:

> There was an old woman of Westward Ho
>   With a hey . . .
> There was an old woman of Westward Ho,
> And over the sea her sons did go.
>   Singing, I will be true. . . .

After that, anything can be made to happen. The fact that the last line of the refrain has little to do with the poem need not trouble anyone. The purpose of giving the refrain as a framework is that most children do not compose readily in rhyme and metre, and filling out their couplets in this way gives size and shape to their efforts. If they are able, of course, let them compose their own refrains, as well as the 'folk-songs' that go with them.

Another good verse exercise is to compose a new set of rhymes for *Old Joe Braddle-um*, which begins:

> Number One, Number One,
> Now my song has just begun,
>   *With a rum–tum–taddle-um,*
>   *Old Joe Braddle-um,*
>   *Eh! what country folks we be.*

After that it is necessary to find a rhyme for each number in turn:

> Number Two, Number Two,
> Some likes a pudding, but I likes a stew.

Such exercises give useful practice in the technique of verse composition; they help to sharpen the wits and stimulate the imagination. The most valuable kind of poetic composition, of course, is the free making of poems on any and every subject that appeals to children, and for this it is impossible to give directions. Showing suitable pictures and playing gramophone records of carefully chosen music may touch off the poetic impulse. Many children will, however, find their best stimulus in nature itself, in their homes, or in the streets of their town.[1]

If children enjoy their poetry lessons, as they should, they will want to try their hands at composition—not always or often, but sometimes at least. Measurable results are not to be expected from verse composition as from working out sums in Arithmetic. The teacher is likely to ask himself occasionally whether he is not, in fact, simply wasting time. But if he re-collects that the composition of competent verses, let alone the making of a poem, is most difficult and exacting, even for a child with unusual verbal skill, he need not be discouraged; every attempt that children make to create something of their own, however imperfect, is a step towards self-fulfilment and away from inertia and acquiescence under the pressure of mass commercial entertainment.

[1] Suggestions for exercises in verse composition are contained in Chapters VIII and XI of the author's *Man Friday: An Introduction to English Composition and Grammar* (Heinemann).

CHAPTER 5

THE SECONDARY SCHOOL: FIRST STAGE

(*11 to 13 Years Old*)

THE recommendations made in the two following chapters on poetry in the secondary school can be applied only loosely so far as the different age-groups are concerned. We have to consider, broadly speaking, the lower half and the upper half of the school, and between these halves, where poetry is concerned, there is a gulf. Experience shows that children of eleven to twelve can be treated as older juniors—no radically different methods are called for, only an increased range of material. They will respond readily to the right poems taught in the right way.

The gulf which occurs about the age of twelve is a complex phenomenon. In the first place, it affects boys, not girls; secondly, it affects the reactions of boys to all aesthetic matters. It is, indeed, a part of the attitude which boys of this age begin to adopt to the opposite sex generally: they become aware of a gulf between themselves and girls, and hence between themselves and poetry, because they regard poetry as in itself something for girls. This attitude does not necessarily extend over music and art, but most teachers will agree that it hampers the teaching of poetry, especially in single-sex schools. Further consideration of this fact must be left to the next chapter.

Another factor which makes the teaching of poetry in secondary schools difficult is the range of ability likely to occur in any one class. In writing of pupils in secondary schools I have in mind those of average ability—that is, not grammar school pupils specifically, nor the 'C', 'D' and 'E' streams of modern schools. I am thinking in general of the more able children in a modern school. But in an educational system in which children are graded according to intelligence, it is unimportant, for poetry teaching, to differentiate between types of school and types of pupil. Intelligence, as measured by such things as intelligence tests, mathematical ability, and even skill in verbal expression, is only one factor, and not necessarily the most important one, in the appreciation of poetry. If we make a theoretical arrangement of all poetry in a scale, with sensuous appeal and rhetoric and simple emotion at one end, and intellectual complexity, including learned allusions, at the other, no doubt we should find that the older pupils in grammar schools could advance further along the scale than those in modern schools. But that does not imply that both categories of pupil could not go a certain distance along the scale, as it were hand in hand, until the point where the less intelligent child was obliged to give up. The pupil in a grammar school might be slightly ahead of his contemporary in a modern school, but only slightly; and in any case not so far ahead as the 'A' stream child in a modern school as compared with the 'E' stream child. Mere intelligibility in poetry is of secondary importance, unless the teacher makes what I would consider exaggerated use of it for the purpose of paraphrase and other more or less intellectual exercises. What is important in gauging the suitability of particular poems for particular children is not the intelligence of the children but their emotional age and their degree of sophistication. In some respects, from the point of view of what I might call 'poetic age', as distinct from mental age or reading age, a boy in a secondary modern school may actually be more advanced than his contemporary in a grammar school. He may begin to find poems babyish which the other can still enjoy.

In this matter of poetic age girls are both older and younger than boys of the same physical age. They are usually more emotionally mature, but their form of sophistication does not involve a violent rejection of poetry as babyish. They not only respond to more mature kinds of poem, they also retain a love of poems they enjoyed when younger. They do not reject, say, *Goblin Market* on account of the goblins while enjoying *The Forsaken Merman* or *The High Tide on the Coast of Lincolnshire* for its more adult emotional appeal.

For practical purposes, then, children of both sexes and all mental ages may be treated alike in the first two years at the secondary school. The teacher will make his own individual adjustments according to his estimate of his pupils' poetic age. This will depend on factors outside their personal development —chiefly, the extent and quality of the poetic education they have received at the primary school. It would be pleasant to assume that all had received something like the training outlined in previous chapters. We should then know just where we were, and could proceed accordingly. Certainly it is hoped that teachers in secondary schools will have read the earlier chapters. But so far as the children are concerned, it is practical to consider a new start. Except in districts where virtually a whole class moves from the top of one primary school to the bottom of a secondary school, we are obliged to regard the lowest form in a secondary school as an entirely new grouping, with little or no poetic education in common. In the present haphazard and chaotic state of poetry teaching, it is certain that some of the class will have been well taught and have a real love of the subject, while others will have been badly taught and are at best indifferent; a third group will have been taught next to no poetry at all and may be prepared to embark on it as a new and special interest associated with their change of school. For most of these, then, a new start.

The only essential difference between the first secondary year and the last primary year is that, where classes consist half, or wholly, of boys, special pains must be taken to keep out of the syllabus poems that might be thought childish. Speech-rhymes should still be practised, somewhat in the spirit of a game, but a game with a definite end in view—clarity and expressiveness of utterance. Children should be encouraged to criticize one another—not with the object of scoring off others, or pillorying defective speech, but because, on the whole, children are fair, keen and observant critics of one another. In any case, the size of classes is likely to preclude the possibility of much individual speech work, and practice will probably be in the form of group activity, so that the class will be called on, as a whole, to comment on the performances, not of individuals, but of groups.

Practice with speech-rhymes will lead naturally to choral speech, the ideal method for enjoying actively such poems as folk-songs with refrains, sea-shanties and narrative ballads with clearly distinguished 'parts' for different speakers or groups.

A beginning might be made with Bunyan's *Pilgrim's Song*, 'Who would true valour see.' This will be known to many as a hymn, and its familiarity may make it welcome. But some hymn-books print an adapted version—the teacher of poetry should use only Bunyan's original text.

> Who would true valour see,
>   Let him come hither;
> One here will constant be,
>   Come wind, come weather.
> There's no discouragement
> Shall make him once relent
> His first avow'd intent
>   To be a pilgrim.
>
> Whoso beset him round
>   With dismal stories,
> Do but themselves confound,
>   His strength the more is.
> No lion can him fright,
> He'll with a giant fight,
> But he will have a right
>   To be a pilgrim.
>
> Hobgoblin nor foul fiend
>   Can daunt his spirit;

> He knows he at the end
>> Shall life inherit.
> Then fancies flee away!
> He'll fear not what men say;
> He'll labour night and day
>> To be a pilgrim.

The poem can be spoken in unison or divided into parts for several voices or groups. In particular, the lines 'No lion can him fright' and 'He'll with a giant fight' would be the more effective for being given to different voices. This is a poem which might well be introduced by a short discussion of bravery: What actions would be considered brave nowadays? What actions were thought brave in the past? Another word for bravery—courage, fearlessness, valour. Has anyone heard a poem about valour? After Bunyan's lines are read, another brief discussion—what actions would still be thought brave? Not fighting with hobgoblins or lions, but refusing to be frightened by imaginary evils. What does the writer mean by 'being a pilgrim?' But it would be a mistake to labour the exact meaning of every line. The poem is essentially a hymn to courage; its strong and resolute rhythm is almost as much a part of its total meaning as is the sense of the words. So the appreciation of the poem should conclude in a vigorous and thoughtful reading aloud.

As a contrast, the ballad of *Sir Eglamore* gives an admirable picture of mock valour. Let the class read the poem first to themselves, and then question them to see if they have understood the irony. Was Sir Eglamore really valiant? Was he altogether a fool? By what trick did he kill the dragon? By what action did he prove himself a coward in the end? When the class have understood the spirit of the joke, let them suggest the manner in which the ballad should be spoken—that is, with a good deal of derision in the voice.

Other ballads which they will enjoy are *The Raggle-Taggle Gypsies*, *High Barbary*, *The Golden Vanity*, and *The Death of Admiral Benbow*. The first of these is spirited and adventurous, the second somewhat grim, the last two tragic. All are vigorous, and lend themselves to active interpretation. At least three of them give scope for discussion, in simple terms, of a human situation—was the lady right to run off with the gypsies? What made her do it? In what way was the behaviour of Benbow in contrast to that of his admirals? And in *The Golden Vanity* there is a story of some psychological complexity—was the cabin-boy entirely to be pitied, or is there a possible defence for the captain's action? Had the cabin-boy an unquestionable right to bargain with his skipper when the ship was in danger?

It must be stressed that such discussions of the content of poems with children of only eleven or so should be no more than a subsidiary activity, intended to increase interest in the poems themselves, not distract from it by turning appreciation into general discussion. A poem must be treated always as a total experience, not simply a verse paraphrase of some prose idea. The greater part of the poetic content—rhythm and language, vigour of style and presentation—can only be appreciated *directly* at this stage—by performance, reading aloud, acting—not critically, through discussion and paraphrase. The main aim to keep in mind is that children should participate in the poetic experience in as much of its variety as possible.

It is sometimes objected to the choice of such poems as have been mentioned that they are songs, and as such are often learned in the music lesson. I cannot see that this is bad. Teachers of singing do not usually have time to consider fully the words of all the songs they teach, and if some of these are studied for their own sake in poetry lessons, surely the enjoyment of both words and melody will be increased. The criterion for the poetry teacher must be the value of the words as poetry—that and nothing else. No such objection, however, can be made to Hardy's *We be the King's Men* and *The Night of Trafalgar*, for although these are clearly songs, there are no generally accepted musical settings.

It is not suggested that the poetry syllabus for this or any other year should consist entirely of ballads or narrative verse.

On the contrary, it is important that the simpler kind of lyric should be introduced, for here feelings are involved more directly; indeed, it is for this very reason that some teachers shy away from, or altogether neglect, lyric poetry. The most universal emotions which have inspired lyric poetry are love, and sorrow at the death of a loved one. It would be unsuitable to read love poems or laments with a class of eleven-year-olds. But love of the opposite sex is only one aspect of love—there is also the love of nature and the love of country and, more generally, wonder and delight at the beauty of visible creation. In the ballads we have action, in lyrics feeling. Is it because boys are interested too exclusively in the literature of action, as distinct from that of thought and feeling, that, compared with girls, they are emotionally immature? At all events, it cannot be denied that lyric poetry is one of the most potent means for the education of the emotions, and it would be a misfortune if it were neglected. Some of the simpler poems of W. H. Davies, Clare, Blake and Hardy can be appreciated by both boys and girls at the beginning of the secondary course. These, in contrast to ballads, are quiet, contemplative, undramatic, yet not the less vivid and memorable. The anonymous song *Poor Old Horse* (not usually sung in music lessons) might be compared with Davies's *The Rabbit*, as exemplifying two ways of writing about the treatment of animals.

Comic or nonsense verse by such writers as Lear and Lewis Carroll should be read and enjoyed for its own sake. At its best it combines action and description with feeling. The feeling or emotion common to all good comic verse is the sense of fun, the enjoyment of the incongruous, the absurd, the unusual. The taste for nonsense is sophisticated and civilized, and not all children possess it. But if they can enjoy *The Lobster Quadrille* or *The Owl and the Pussycat*, they will have learnt to appreciate poetry in one of its most engaging moods.

I have mentioned earlier the value of getting children to make drawings to illustrate poems, and of learning by heart lines that they have enjoyed. Of the greatest importance, too, at this stage is the writing of original verse as a complementary activity to reading the poetry of others. Children vary greatly in their capacity to turn out rhymed and rhythmical verses, and clearly no great achievement is to be expected. Most immature poetry is written in imitation, direct or remote, of some poem which has appealed to the writer. Whenever some poem that has been studied in class seems to have had more than the usual appeal, it is worth while trying to get the class to make up poems of their own in a similar style or on a similar theme. The creative instinct is, in its simplest form, nothing but the desire, the impulse to make something of one's own as an expression of the pleasure one has got from experiencing the creation of another. It is often sufficient to tell a class to read such-and-such a poem or poems and afterwards to try to make up one of their own. No direction need be given as to how much, or how little to copy; and the results should not be judged according to the degree of their 'originality'.

I will end this chapter by recommending a practice I have found fruitful, throughout the secondary years, in stimulating original writing.

I once read with a class of eleven-year-old boys a simple Chinese poem in Arthur Waley's translation on the subject of Homecoming. Here it is.

> At fifteen I went with the army,
> At fourscore I came home.
> On the way I met a man from the village,
> I asked him who there was at home.
> 'That over there is your house,
> All covered over with trees and bushes.'
> Rabbits had run in at the dog-hole,
> Pheasants flew down from the beams of the roof.
> In the courtyard was growing some wild grain;
> And by the well, some wild mallows.
> I'll boil the grain and make porridge,
> I'll pluck the mallows and make soup.
> Soup and porridge are both cooked,

But there is no one to eat them with.
I went out and looked towards the east,
While tears fell and wetted my clothes.

Something about the poem aroused more than the usual interest: perhaps it was the simplicity of statement, the bald 'unpoetic language', the obvious truth of the feeling, or just the unusual form, the free verse. So I suggested that the class should write free-verse poems of their own on the same subject —Homecoming. I gave them a quarter of an hour. The results were interesting. Here is one of them.

The boy came out of school
When he came home
The door was locked
He asked the next door neighbour
Where his mother was.
She had gone out so he sat down and cried.
After a long time his mother came home
He ran with outstretched arms to meet her.

I quote this, not as being good poetry, but as being a successful attempt at self-expression within definite time- and subject-limits, by an average boy with no special aptitude. Some of the results were poetically better than this, others not so good. The brief example just quoted has the merit of completeness; the form suggested by the Chinese 'model' was evidently just right, for this boy, as a means of recapturing and re-creating an experience which must have been of some emotional significance.

This is not, as I have said, a remarkable poem, but it is good writing: and that is what matters. Let us call it good prose—it is at least simple, sincere and straightforward. It contains none of the faults usually found in juvenile prose composition. The usual subjects set for prose composition do not encourage the kind of simplicity and directness here exhibited, because the demand to write 'sentences' is too vague for the immature. Prose develops in the history of a nation centuries after verse,

and the construction of a 'correct' prose paragraph, or even
sentence, makes severe demands on the immature. But let them
write verse, and the problems of syntax, construction and
balance solve themselves, or disappear. There is no better training for writing of any sort than the writing of verse. Name
almost any of the good English prose writers, and you realize
that most of them served their apprenticeship in verse (some
of course, going further than mere apprenticeship). Defoe,
Addison, Johnson, Swift, Goldsmith, Lamb, Borrow—the list
can be lengthened almost indefinitely. Only Bacon, Hazlitt
and Shaw, so far as I can discover, achieved success by another
route. There is no linguistic discipline like the composing of
verses; but for the average child the mere mechanics of metre
and rhyme are in many cases an insuperable difficulty. The
writing of conventional verse should certainly, however, be
attempted; and with practice it becomes easier. But as an
occasional relief from technical difficulties, free-verse composition is invaluable.

Children like to achieve results; they value the feeling of
having created something of their own, whole and unaided.
This is generally understood by progressive teachers of art, but
teachers of English have not been so quick to grasp it. A line
of free verse, much more than a prose sentence, can become the
unit of thought, the vehicle for expressing a variable amount of
observation or feeling. I should not quarrel with anyone who
maintained that the above examples of free verse *are* prose in
all but typographical lay-out. The approach is different. The
mere demand to break up the thought in this way acts as a
check on vagueness and rambling; it gives free play to a latent
sense of verbal rhythm; it encourages brevity and succinctness;
but above all, the feeling that what is being written is *poetry* of
a sort, not simply narrative or description, is a spur to creative
expression: the lines are there for what they *are*, not only for
what they say.

In writing free verse there can be complete freedom in the
choice of subject-matter. It will not always be necessary to

provide 'models'. Sometimes it is enough simply to give a word, such as 'blue', and ask the class to write free-verse poems about as many 'blue' things as they can think of. Blue skies, blue flowers, blue books, blue eyes—these are the obvious things to expect, but there will always be surprises, even in the efforts of the most apparently unimaginative children. It is as if the mere thought of the colour-epithet acted as a selective magnet drawing out of the child's unconscious all sorts of memories, and suggesting connections he could never have consciously made.

When 'models' are used—that is, when poems are used as a starting-point for original work—they are intended to provide a stimulus, to stir up the dormant imaginative processes. It is not likely that any children will actually copy a 'model', in the plagiaristic sense. It must always be remembered that we are dealing with immature, unformed minds—minds in the act of drawing nourishment from the world around, including the world of art and literature—and that real originality is not to be expected. Imitation is the natural way to maturity and self-dependence. Most poets, even the greatest, remain imitators long after they reach our present school leaving age. Our task is not to discourage imitation, but rather to encourage the kind of imitation that will best help towards self-development.

It is because of its value in assisting in this task that I have written at length about free verse as a model for original work. Briefly, it offers the right balance between freedom and restraint. It is hardly necessary to add that the abler children will readily compose also poems of more conventional form, regular in metre and rhyme.

The reading and writing of free verse can go on throughout the secondary course. A class of intelligent fourteen-year-old boys were on one occasion much impressed by D. H. Lawrence's *Bat*, a poem highly irregular in form, even for free verse. I suggested they should write one of their own on any other animal. No time-limit was imposed. Among a number of successful imitations, the following was one of the best. I must leave it to the reader to judge whether the boy's imagination was restricted or liberated by reading Lawrence's poem.

ROOKS

A black shape glides in front of the sun,
What is it?
A cloud?
What can it be?
There it is!
Hovering over that patch of scrub,
Could it be a hawk?
Another joins it. What are they?
Rooks!
I know them by their yellow beaks, like pointed hammers.
Their wings are like torn black sheets.
There's one, after a rabbit.
He's got it.
Murderer!
Ah! it's dusk now.
They swoop back to their rookeries,
A hundred feet above the ground,
Where nobody can get at them.
Rooks!

This was written by an 'A'-stream grammar school boy. In case teachers of less intelligent children find this fact discouraging, let me quote from a bulletin I have just received describing work on an experimental syllabus carried out with ordinary children in New Zealand. 'The writing of poetry by children', the report runs, 'has been one of the most successful things in the trial syllabus work. It is remarkable that some apparently non-literary children have found in this their most satisfying form of written expression.'

CHAPTER 6

THE SECONDARY SCHOOL: SECOND STAGE

(*13 to 15 Years Old*)

IN the previous chapter I spoke of the gulf which occurs in the aesthetic development of boys at the age of twelve or thirteen. The bridging of this gulf is one of the most difficult, and at the same time important, problems to be faced by a teacher of poetry. In a school where boys will continue their education until eighteen, perhaps with the intention of going on to a university, it would be reasonable to teach little poetry between thirteen and sixteen; in the sixth form boys will return to it with increased maturity and fresh interest. But with the great majority of children, who will have little or no formal education after fifteen, we cannot do this. To neglect such an important part of a boy's or girl's aesthetic education as the appreciation of poetry in the last two years of school life can—and too often does—bring about permanent emotional impoverishment. What we have to try to do, then, is to give those who are going to leave at fifteen at least some acquaintance with most of the great English poets from Chaucer to the present day.

This chapter is concerned more with the choice of poems than with methods of teaching: if the former is right, the latter must be left largely to the skill and judgement of the teacher. It is perfectly possible for a dull teacher to murder a masterpiece, but it is doubtful if this is more harmful than to drag unwilling boys of fourteen through second-rate and third-rate counterfeit poetry. I believe that if a teacher has some personal enthusiasm for the best in poetry, he will find the means to convey his enthusiasm to even the most reluctant adolescents.

71

If he has no enthusiasm, he had better not be teaching poetry. A teacher once asked me, with complete sincerity, what I would advise him to do when, with no personal enthusiasm for the subject, he was obliged to teach poetry to boys in a secondary school. I told him that in those circumstances the best I could suggest was that he should provide the class with some good poetry books and let them read to themselves; if after a while he got them to talk to him about what they had discovered, perhaps they would convey to him some of their own enthusiasm. Such a practice, though not recommended as ideal, would at least do no harm.

Provided the choice of poems is right, the criterion in judging the validity of a method at this stage is whether or not it succeeds in arousing interest. If *The Ancient Mariner* bores a class of fourteen-year-olds, it is being badly taught. Scope must be allowed for variety and unconventionality in method—even for eccentricity. If after he has left school a boy remembers *Paradise Lost* because he is convinced that his teacher was mad, that is a vindication of the teacher's methods. Indeed, the nature of poetry is such that the good teacher may well be the one with some madness in his method.

A young man once began his career as an English master at one of our rougher boys' secondary schools by informing the headmaster that he proposed to do a production of *Macbeth*. The headmaster, in an effort to dissuade him, told him to reconsider this revolutionary project with the utmost care and return in a week's time and tell him if he still thought it wise. A week later the young man duly reported on his deliberations. 'You're quite right, sir,' he said. 'I've decided not to do *Macbeth*. It'll be *Romeo and Juliet*.' This illustrates the point I have been insisting on, that what matters is the quality of the material chosen and the enthusiasm of the teacher.

There is no single problem more important for the English teacher than the choice of poems for adolescents—unless it is the choice of anything else on the aesthetic plane. For education is the training of taste; and there is a sense in which everything—from simple nourishment to complex behaviour—is ultimately a matter of taste. From the moment he is weaned, a child begins to exercise the power of choice. As he grows, the range of possible choice expands; primitive man, living by necessity and custom, has little individual freedom of choice. Civilized man exercises an immense power of choice in all directions.

We cannot reason out every choice; we may choose by habit, or by instinct: trained instinct is taste. The more choices material civilization offers, the more important becomes the training of taste as an end in education. A boy who has learned to speak and behave pleasingly without effort is one whose taste in speech and conduct has been well trained; a girl who has learned to dress pleasingly and make the most of her appearance is one who has somehow acquired taste in matters of appearance. Of course, a good education will attempt to give an all-round training in taste—that is, an instinctive aptitude for choosing the best and most becoming in all things.

There is no evidence that children have naturally good taste in anything. Little boys prefer to behave noisily and ostentatiously, little girls prefer gaudy and inharmonious colours; both prefer sweet, highly-flavoured food to what is wholesome and nourishing. At the present time they are particularly open to the influence of the specious and the counterfeit, both in food and in entertainment. So skilful are the purveyors of the specious that it is unwise to assume that children will acquire good habits of taste without active efforts by parents and teachers. The analogy between food and the arts is a fair one, and is useful within limits. The very use of the word 'taste' is suggestive. Now in education the enemy of the good is not so much the downright bad as the counterfeit. The marks of the counterfeit are that it is superficially more attractive, that it is easily assimilated, and that it is parasitic on the good. This last is the most important: for if we lose the power to distinguish the counterfeit from the good, we lose all sense of value, and the good may be lost to us. The notorious remark of a Minister of Food that butter could not be distinguished from margarine was, ultimately, an immoral statement. Margarine is counterfeit butter—its very form is determined by the traditional form of butter: there is no natural reason why we should eat coconuts disguised as a smooth yellow paste; custard powder is counterfeit eggs; spiced sauces are a disguise for tasteless and unappetizing food; silver paper and transparent wrappings are a disguise for basically dull processed foods.

Here the analogy must end. Art is much more complicated and debatable. England produces the best poetry and some of the best food in the world; and the badness of some English cooking may be not unconnected with English failures in aesthetic judgement. The point to be made is that the bad, in the aesthetic sense, is an imitation of the good; we cannot be content that children should subsist on imitations. It is often said that there is no disputing about tastes: on the contrary, there is much dispute. The more interesting and important the object of taste, the more dispute. That there is no final conclusion to the dispute is another matter. No teacher should dogmatize irrationally about what is or is not a good poem; on the other hand, he should be able to see for himself what is the genuine article and what gives a cracked ring when dropped on the counter. But he cannot, like a booking-clerk, just throw away the counterfeit coin; he must supply something in its place. He must realize that the worst is a corruption of the best; disentangle the good elements, see where they have become falsified, and place them once more in their proper setting.

It might be thought that all thinking teachers of English had discarded the false coinage that was current in the anthologies of a generation ago, and replaced them by sound currency. It might be thought that romantic highwaymen, Sherwood in the twilight, the drunken private of the Buffs, the good news brought to Aix, Sennacherib, Lochinvar, have fallen into ignominious disuse. But the regularity with which they are still reprinted in the very latest school poetry books suggests several things. First, their opponents may have exclaimed too loudly and derisively against them, thus inviting a sympathetic reaction in their favour; secondly, the force of habit and tradition among anthologists is strong; thirdly, there may be something in these poems after all.

First: mere derision is useless. Of course, to an enlightened reader of *How They Brought the Good News*, Messrs. Sellar and Yeatman's parody may be an adequate answer:

I sprang to the rollocks and Jorrocks and me,
And I galloped, you galloped, he galloped, we galloped all three . . .
Not a word to each other, we kept changing place,
Neck to neck, back to front, ear to ear, face to face.

But destructive criticism alone is not sufficient. Exactly why is the original poem funny? If you cannot critically evaluate it, you have no real answer to the sturdy conservative who says, 'I was brought up on it. The boys like it; and anyway, what's wrong with it?'

Secondly, if a poem has appeared in the anthologies for a generation or more, strong reasons must be given for displacing it. Otherwise the established poems that happen to be good may be thrown out too, and poetry teaching become a mere matter of fashion. The weakest point about school anthologies is their habit of inbreeding; most of them suggest that their compilers have read little poetry except what appears in school anthologies. When a new collection such as Messrs. Auden and Garrett's *The Poet's Tongue* shows evidence of wide reading outside the usual range, its success may be immediate. Moreover, the old favourite (such as *The High Tide on the Coast of Lincolnshire*) is read to new advantage in a new setting. The thinking teacher begins to ask himself, 'Why do they include this poem, when so many that usually go with it are omitted?'

Thirdly, there is always the argument: The children like it. The answer: Have you tried seeing if they like anything else? is not altogether satisfactory. Granted the fact that children prefer ice-cream and fish and chips to more wholesome food, we have to admit that an excess of these is better than an unsatisfied hunger; and that a dull diet may lead to loss of appetite. We must find out why these counterfeit poems—for such I believe them to be—appeal to adolescents, and how we ought to replace them, if we believe in training taste.

The argument is sometimes heard: I used to love such-and-such a poem as a child; of course I've grown out of it now, but it didn't do me any harm. Too often the adult who has grown out of his school poems has grown out of all poetry; and the present state of poetic taste—the unprecedented lack of general interest in the whole subject—may be due partly to wrong teaching. There is no good evidence that the poetic teaching of twenty or thirty years ago has produced anything other than a reaction against all poetry in later years. In other cases the speaker is a sophisticated reader who can appreciate the memory of *Barbara Frietchie* while still preferring Hopkins. But he is a rare exception.

Yet people who now read no poetry can still remember with pleasure their Newbolt and Noyes. They can now recognize a counterfeit poem and reject it, but still their affections cling round childhood memories and associations. Is not this the strongest argument for giving them only the best at school? For if this best be of a quality such as can still appeal to their maturer judgement, may they not retain and increase the love of poetry, instead of rejecting it altogether as a childish folly? If, as I believe, English taste in music at present is infinitely better developed and more widely practised than poetic taste— whatever the sufferers in hospitals forced to listen all day to the Light Programme may think—this is perhaps due to the fact that on the whole school music is of a higher standard than school poetry, and more enthusiastically and more entertainingly taught. This is due largely to the efforts of Cecil Sharp at the Board of Education fifty years ago. Poetry has not had its Sharp; and inspectors of schools, however energetically they report on bad sanitation, allow the most trashy poetry books, especially in primary schools, to pass without comment. We do not want dictators of taste, but in some cases, perhaps, they might suggest with more ardour.

For what reasons do counterfeit poems appeal to adolescents? They are usually found to possess one or more of the following elements: a rousing story; an obvious rhythm; a glamorized view of life; a crude emotional appeal. In all these there is bad and good—or if not good, at any rate something we must take account of. Take the last first: if we read Sir Francis Doyle's *The Private of the Buffs*, we see that its main appeal is that of a crude and false patriotism—patriotism degraded into racialism.

> Let Dusky Indians whine and kneel:
> An English lad must die.

Exasperated by this sort of sentiment—it is hard to say whether the first or the second line is the more offensive—the sensitive reader may infer that all patriotic poetry is bad, even that all patriotism is bad. This is not so; and it would be a pity if a natural distaste for jingoism blinded us to the appeal of genuine patriotic poetry to adolescents. Patriotism is good in poetry if it is simple and unpretentious, or if it does not take itself too seriously. The latter sort was written in Elizabethan times (Drayton's *Agincourt*) and the Regency (Marryat's *The Old Navy*); an example of simple, inoffensive and deeply felt patriotic emotion is Hardy's *The Night of Trafalgar*.

> In the wild October night-time, when the wind raved round the land,
> And the Back-sea met the Front-sea, and our doors were blocked with sand,
> And we heard the drub of Dead-man's Bay, where bones of thousands are,
> We knew not what the day had done for us at Trafalgár.

Put beside this Newbolt's popular *Admirals All*, and the hollowness of the latter is immediately evident.

> Effingham, Grenville, Raleigh, Drake—
> Here's to the bold and free.

(In what sense, one cannot help asking, was Raleigh 'free'?)

> Benbow, Collingham, Byron, Blake—
> Hail to the kings of the sea!

It is a mere jingle of names; and in the whole poem the mechanical sing-song of the rhythm is as empty as the underlying theme, that naval warfare is a carefree, dashing, piratical adventure. It reminds one of another characteristic line from Newbolt:

> For we're all in love with fighting on the Fighting Temeraire!

What naval rating on any ship, at any time, could possibly have been supposed to give vent to such an irresponsible and unrealistic sentiment?

But is there no such thing as heroism in the navy? Is no sea-fight a fitting subject for poetry for boys? To read the moving anonymous popular ballad of the early eighteenth century, *The Death of Admiral Benbow*, is at once to know the sound and taste of the real thing.

> Says Kirby unto Wade, we will run, we will run,
> Says Kirby unto Wade, we will run;
> For I value no disgrace, nor the losing of my place,
> But the enemy I won't face, nor his guns, nor his guns. . . .
>
> Brave Benbow lost his legs by chain-shot, by chain-shot,
> Brave Benbow lost his legs by chain-shot:
> Brave Benbow lost his legs, and all on his stumps he begs—
> Fight on my English lads, 'tis our lot, 'tis our lot.

As a story, *How They Brought the Good News* is sheer bluff—a piece of pseudo-historical make-believe which cannot bear examination: neither God nor Robert Browning knew what the good news was. My own belief is that Aix had had a bad harvest and run out of wine, so that Joris and Co. were sent to Ghent to negotiate a deal with the local vintners; this was brought off just as the last barrel of inferior Aix wine was reached. However, the thinness of the story is forgotten in the excitement of the ride, reflected in the stirring but mechanical anapaests; and in the glamorized, glittering, streamlined surface of the poem. It is really a poem exploiting the popularity of that noble animal, the horse; but Roland is not real—he is the Metro-Goldwyn horse of popular imagination, going through all its circus tricks. But is not the horse a noble animal, and is sentimentality about horses among the adolescent to be banned entirely? The horse is, indeed, noble, and his nobility has been incomparably evoked by the writer of the Book of Job; or if the heart is truly to be touched about a horse, let it be the *Poor Old Horse* of the traditional song.

My clothing was once of the linsey-wolsey fine,
My tail it grew at length, my coat did likewise shine;
Now I am growing old; my beauty does decay,
My master frowns upon me: one day I heard him say,
    Poor old horse: poor old horse. . . .

'You are old, you are cold, you are deaf, dull, dumb and slow,
You are not fit for anything, or in my team to draw.
You have eaten all my hay, you have spoilt all my straw,
So hang him, whip, stick him, to the huntsman let him go.'
    Poor old horse: poor old horse.

Scott, I think, was the originator of phoney historical episodes in verse, with glossy surfaces and a slick movement. *Lochinvar* is rattling good fun, with plenty of neat phrases to thrill the immature reader. But would it not be worth while to compare it with the original Border ballad from which it was lifted? Here are the relevant verses from *Katherine Johnstone*.

'O come ye here to fight, young Lord?
    Or come ye here to play?
Or come ye here to drink good wine
    Upon the weddin'-day?'

'I come na here to fight,' he said,
    'I come na here to play;
I'll but lead a dance wi' the bonny bride,
    And mount and go my way.'

There was a glass of blude-red wine
   Was fill'd them up between,
But aye she drank to Lamington
   Who her true love had been.

He's ta'en her by the milk-white hand,
   And by the grass-green sleeve;
He's mounted her high behind himsel',
   And her kin he speired na leave.

There were four and twenty bonny boys
   A' clad in Johnstone grey,
They swore they would tak' the bride again
   By the strong hand if they may.

It's up, it's up the Cowden bank
   It's down the Cowden brae;
The bride she gar'd the trumpet sound
   'It is a weel won play!'

The blude ran down by Cowden bank
   And down by Cowden brae,
But aye she gar'd the trumpet sound,
   'It's a' fair play!'

'My blessing on your heart, sweet thing!
   Wae to your wilfu' will!
Sae mony a gallant gentleman's blood
   This day as ye've gar'd spill.'

Further exercises for thinking readers might be to consider the quality of Noyes's *Sherwood* after reading some of the traditional Robin Hood ballads, and to decide whether there is implied racialism in *He Fell Among Thieves*.

It must be remembered by the sophisticated that, while all is not gold that glisters, we must not undervalue real gold, or honest copper, or expect the young to do without it. What we are on the look-out for is false emotion, slick technique, bombast and unreality. These are most likely to occur when literary men write about the life of action, and men with axes to grind borrow the tools of poetry. 'Romance' and 'glamour' are two of the most abused words in popular culture, but the fact that their appeal to the young has been exploited by the writers of counterfeit poetry should not be allowed to interfere with our appreciation of the glamour (which only means 'magic') of real heroism and endurance, and the romance some-times associated with the life of action, its pathos as well as its triumphs.

> I dug his grave with a silver spade,
> *To my way, stormalong!*
> I dug his grave with a silver spade,
> *Aye, aye, aye, Mister Stormalong.*
>
> I lowered him down with a golden chain,
> *To my way, stormalong!*
> I lowered him down with a golden chain,
> *Aye, aye, aye, Mister Stormalong.*

The anonymous shanty is as moving as any more pretentious sea-poem by a Georgian literary man; and quite as appealing and memorable when taught to unlettered adolescents.

Given taste and enthusiasm, what lines of approach is the teacher likely to find most profitable for boys and girls aged thirteen to fifteen? The methods suggested for earlier age-groups have been mainly uncritical. At thirteen or so children can be expected to think more critically about poetry—to be interested in its thought and its technique.

To take a simple example: the humane treatment of animals is a subject that will engage the interest of most adolescents. Poems such as the anonymous *Poor Old Horse*, James Stephens's *The Snare* and D. H. Lawrence's *Two Performing Elephants* can be discussed for their content alone. Purists will object that poetry is not propaganda; nor is it. But no one can deny that many poems contain an element of propaganda and rightly

D

involve humanitarian feelings. It is not a disservice to poetry to isolate and discuss the element of propaganda, though it would be wrong to teach that this is its only, or even its principal, aim.

Children of thirteen might well be asked to consider the idea contained in such a prose paraphrase as the following:

> The birds pattered on my roof with a quiet soothing sound like rain; but not even this was enough to make me forget the rabbit caught in an iron trap. For throughout the night he cries out in agony, until, with a smile of triumph, a man with a knife comes in the morning to murder him.

Having discussed this, they can then be introduced to Davies's original poem *The Rabbit*, and asked to say which is the more effective—paraphrase or poem.

> Not even when the early birds
> Danced on my roof with showery feet
> Such music as will come from rain—
> Not even then could I forget
> The rabbit in his hours of pain;
> Where, lying in an iron trap,
> He cries all through the deafened night—
> Until his smiling murderer comes,
> To kill him in the morning light.

In this way one of the purposes or virtues of poetry is illustrated, and the discussion turns from the propagandist to the technical aspect. The verse is, clearly, more striking and memorable. Here the function of rhythmical utterance is hinted at, and a direct experience of the heightened emotional power of rhythm and rhyme is gained. There is, of course, a danger of suggesting that poetry is simply metrical prose: it must not be implied that the poet had in his mind, before writing the poem, some such prose statement as was given first. It must be explained that the prose is merely an approximation to the thought, the idea of the poem, and in no way a substitute for it. However, it is admittedly impossible to prevent most people from regarding poetry, at some time or another, as metrified prose. The danger is less if they have been given a 'poetic' approach to poetry from the start; if, that is, they have been taught to enjoy the sound and rhetoric as a total experience, without troubling prematurely about the thought.

At a later stage—fourteen or fifteen—an example of a poem embodying a 'message' is Shelley's sonnet *Ozymandias*. Here it is clearly relevant to take the poem as propaganda against temporal power, an imaginative statement of the feelings aroused by the contemplation of tyranny.

A more sustained poem with a 'message' is Gray's *Elegy*, which also is based on the idea of the vanity of worldly power and success. The mature reader knows that there is much more in it than this; but the political implications of the poem—its radicalism, its attack on privilege—may be what first arouses the interest of the adolescent.

A consideration of the content of a poem may lead in two directions, towards distinct but related fields of study: technique and biography.

Asked to consider the mood or tone of the *Elegy*, most children will appreciate that it is 'solemn' or 'sad'. They will then realize that this mood is produced and heightened, not only by the 'Gothic' imagery, but also by the measured movement of the stanzas. Ask them to remove one iambic foot from each line—no very difficult feat for most of the stanzas—and see what difference it makes:

> The curfew tolls the knell of day,
>   The lowing herd winds o'er the lea;
> The ploughman homeward plods his way
>   And leaves the darkening world to me.

The analysis of poems at this stage should not be either elaborate or technical. To over-emphasize the poet's workmanship is to distract interest from the poem as a total experience; while the use of technical expressions, such as the names of metres and the forms of poems, will make the study of poetry seem dry and abstract if it is carried beyond the interest and understanding of the pupil. At the same time, many readers of fourteen will find it useful, and not dull, to have a few technical terms at their command—'iambic', 'sonnet', 'alliteration', 'simile' and 'metaphor' are examples. But the mere identification of figures of speech as an end in itself is futile. Such technical information is best introduced incidentally: it can so easily become a substitute for feeling and insight.

All I have said about poetry and the adolescent is coloured by the recognition that it is not easy to gain and keep the interest of the ordinary child of today. But many who may show little interest in poetry may find greater interest in poets. Most adolescents are interested in people, and on the level of biography a real interest in poetry may be awakened. Mention was made of Shelley's hatred of tyranny, as illustrated in *Ozymandias*. This motive might be taken as the theme of a biographical study of the poet, which could lead to enhanced interest in some at least of his other poems—the *Ode to the West Wind*, for instance, with its passionate expression of the desire for freedom, its protest against earthly restraints. In this way an apparently 'unreal' poem can be related to the common emotions of youth.

Not that biography alone is enough. But some study of the lives of poets such as Milton, Clare, Byron, Keats, Davies and Owen will help to fill in the background to the printed page and implant the notion of the poet as 'a man speaking to men'.

The history of poetry, as such, can hardly form a large part of the English course before the sixth form. But the encouragement of a historical, as well as a critical, sense will help to relate poetry to the general body of the child's growing interests. How the heroic couplet satisfied eighteenth-century notions of formalism in architecture and design generally; how the ballad form of *The Ancient Mariner* was connected with the revival of Gothic in the late eighteenth century; how the long narrative poem responded to the demands of the large middle-class, novel-reading public in the nineteenth century; how the short lyric accorded with Elizabethan domestic habits in music; how the form of the medieval ballad, with its frequent repetitions and metrical regularity, suited a largely non-literate public— such matters cannot be gone into in detail, or be expected to interest ordinary readers of thirteen or so to any great degree. But they can be mentioned in passing and treated as facts showing the connection of poetry with the lives of ordinary people throughout history.

In short, the study of poetry as an activity of wider import than simply a disconnected assemblage of poems can have interest and relevance at this stage. But biography and literary history cannot be treated in isolation from poetry. If they form a part of the teacher's own background knowledge, they will take their proper place in the study of poems.

Finally, let it be remembered that far more adolescents can, and do, write poems than their elders realize. The writing of a poem need not be a more unnatural thing for an adolescent than drawing or painting, essay-writing or solving an equation. Part of the study of poetic technique should be, at least occasionally, the composing of blank verse, ballad stanzas, rhymed quatrains in pentameters (Gray's *Elegy* metre), free verse, or octosyllabic couplets. The subject may be anything in which the writer is interested, and the quantity need not be great. Provided the teacher does not demand a high standard of technical proficiency, and provided he conveys the feeling that he is 'on their side' in regarding the writing of good verse as no easy task, but one requiring patience and thought, he will not be disappointed in the results.

I know of no tricks or 'stunts' for the teaching of verse-composition: it will vary in usefulness from pupil to pupil as a piece of simple vocabulary work or word-manipulation on the one hand to an effort of artistic creation on the other, providing a real outlet for emotion and a release of inner tension. There will always be, in any class, some children who will do it better than others—and these will not necessarily be those whom the teacher would expect to be the best: but they may be just those who are not particularly good at other things, and this implies that the writing of poems satisfies special needs. Incidentally, the willingness to write poems, and give them in, will be one test of the degree of confidence established between teacher and pupil.

PART II

The Wood

––––––––––––––––––––•––––––––––––––––––––

CHAPTER 7

WHY TEACH POETRY?

POETRY is the fruit of a creative activity—call it an art, though in some ways it is less like art than nature, human nature. For humanity is inconceivable without language, and poetry is as old, or nearly as old, as language. Without going into rival theories of the origin of language, we can at least admit that in its most basic form language is intimately connected with the expression of emotion—fear, anger, desire, pleasure, and so on. Poetry arises as soon as language becomes organized, however simply, for the purpose of expressing emotion; and as soon as poetry arises, a new emotion comes into being—pleasure in language; this is the basis of a love for poetry. Poetry comes from the conscious organization of language in a form calculated to give pleasure or satisfaction in itself.

Of the fundamental importance of poetry to primitive societies or to children there can be no doubt. But from primitive beginnings poetry has developed into a highly self-conscious art, and the question arises whether society has not outgrown it. I do not propose to go into this in detail, for there is enough evidence that some adults get pleasure from poetry for us to assume that it would be a good thing if more did so. In any case, I must assume that the reader who has read so far agrees with me about the importance of poetry. It would be best if at this point I admitted openly that far from apologizing for poetry, I am a fanatic for it, and that the reader had better make due allowances. My beliefs may seem extravagant; it is easy to object that, being a poet myself, I am prejudiced. I admit this, but I am prepared to give my reasons. I will do the reader the justice of supposing, however, that he would prefer to read a book about poetry written by a fanatic than by an apologist.

Poetry is to me the supreme expression of the human spirit because of its common, one might almost say commonplace, ingredients: it is made up of language, which is the medium for expressing men's most trivial and everyday thoughts. It is for this very reason that it is supreme. Just as the language of poetry is a refinement, an organization, a selection of the best in everyday language; so poetry itself is a refinement, an organization and a selection of the best in human experience. What poetry does to the mass of ordinary experience is to make permanent and memorable whatever in it is vital and significant. No one can doubt that poetry of a crude and simple form, and often of a beautiful form, is a vital and significant part of the lives of children; it enters into the private play of infants and the group play of older children, almost without exception. Yet by the time children have left school, ninety-nine per cent of them have no use for it. It could easily be maintained that this is because poetry is not felt to be a vital part of the adult life of a modern community. Poetry belongs to a magical view of the world, and the modern world is not regarded as magical. But is this so? There is much evidence in the popular culture of even a modern materialistic community that it still has a need for some sort of magic, that its imagination still dwells on the unknown, which is part of the region of poetry. Moreover, is it not reasonable to maintain that poetry might mean more in the adult world if it had been better taught at school? I believe that a revision of the current attitude to the teaching of poetry might effect a salutary change in the quality of adult culture. This book is written in that belief.

The effectiveness of poetry teaching is due to certain special circumstances. Discounting for the moment the claims I have just made for poetry, suppose we regard it simply as one of the arts, like music and drawing. Both of these arts are taught in schools by specialists—that is, those who have at least a rudimentary talent for their subject, a personal interest in it, and hence a sense of mission. A good, or even an average music teacher can play an instrument, possibly sing as well, and gets personal pleasure from listening to others perform. It is almost inconceivable, in short, that anyone would take up music teaching without some aptitude and interest. The same applies to the teaching of art. I do not wish to imply that all is well with the appreciation of these arts in the adult world, or that they are taught ideally. But they are in a better situation than poetry.

There are no specialist teachers of poetry. Posts are not advertised for poetry teachers. The subject is regarded as a department of English, and the main aim in the teaching of English is to make children literate, to teach them to speak and read correctly, and to give them some power of appreciating prose literature. But the utilitarian aspect comes first—and rightly so, if we give first importance to the training of citizens in a modern commercial community. I am not arguing the rights and wrongs of this; I am stating simply that the position of poetry in the curriculum is made difficult. Accordingly, the teacher of poetry need never have written a line of verse; he may not even derive pleasure from reading it. He may have no special knowledge of it. I am not disparaging teachers of English in general, I am saying what seems to me the truth according to my experience. Countless teachers of English do indeed teach poetry conscientiously as a part of literature not to be neglected, but without any special enthusiasm or aptitude. This is to their credit.

Should there be, then, specialist posts in the teaching of poetry? Not necessarily, for the importance I have claimed for poetry arises, to my mind, precisely from the fact that it is not specialized in the same way as music and drawing. I believe that what is needed is a changed status for poetry in the curriculum, and a changed attitude on the part of English teachers in general.

What I have said about the supremacy of poetry needs some enlargement. In saying that poetry is the supreme cultural activity, I do not mean that all poems are supreme, or that we should read only the supreme poems. On the contrary, one of the mistakes made by teachers of poetry—especially the best teachers—is to concentrate too exclusively on the best poems, the 'great' poems, that is. Because poetry is so important, it is essential that we should not act importantly about it. If it is important, there is room not only for the supreme poems but also for the humbler ones. We should think less of 'greatness' and more of goodness.

This is not to say that we should 'lower our standards', or that we should read poems we know to be bad in order to make children like poetry. In order to be useful, a coinage must contain, not only pound notes, but also silver and copper pieces. The poetry we teach must include, not only Keats's odes and Blake's songs, but also verses of less value, though not necessarily less goodness. There are many kinds of goodness. What we must avoid is false coinage, poems dressed up to sound 'great', sham heroics and insincere emotion. This can only debase the poetic currency and destroy confidence.

The teaching of music or the graphic arts may afford parallels for the consideration of poetry. For what the teaching of poetry lacks is precisely what makes these other arts a more manageable part of the curriculum. In music or drawing there is a generally recognized progression of exercises and other procedures which gives these subjects a practical coherence lacked by poetry as a class subject. Now all that is done, for the most part, in the teaching of poetry is to take successively more difficult poems with each successive class, and teach the children to read, understand and appreciate them. There is, of course, a similar procedure in what is called 'musical appreciation', but it is not usually divorced from sight-reading and singing, not to mention the mastery of some instrument, such as those of the percussion band, the recorder, the piano. Nor does an art teacher offer his classes a succession of pictures, from cave-drawings to the portraits of Augustus John, for appreciation. On the contrary, his lessons are often excessively practical, and the children are expected to be unremittingly 'creative' from their earliest years. If this is to err, it is to err in the right direction. What is needed in teaching any cultural subject is a balanced curriculum, not weighted too heavily on the side of either creation or appreciation.

We attempt to teach children to write by making them write in prose. We should teach them to write verse. My years of teaching poetry were wasted because I did not realize this simple but revolutionary truth soon enough.[1]

One of the main differences between prose and verse is that of concentration: prose is highly diffuse and discursive, verse is more pithy and concentrated. There are, of course, exceptions —the prose of Bacon is more pithy than the verse of Whitman. But, in general, verse is more direct, its form tighter. Prose is, comparatively, relaxed and sophisticated. I have so often heard it said, 'All we want to aim at in the English course is to teach children to write clear, simple prose.' All we want to aim at! But the writing of clear simple prose is what the educated classes in England did not achieve until after centuries of discipline in the study of verse. There is very little prose before Dryden which would satisfy a modern employer on the grounds of clarity and simplicity, but there was good, and great, verse at least two and a half centuries earlier. Clear, simple prose is the final flower of the verbal arts, not something we can expect from a twelve-year-old.

I am certain that what children of twelve ought to be writing is not colourless, though perhaps grammatical, prose

---

[1] A full and carefully documented study of the significance of poetry—and especially the writing of poetry—in the development of children will be found in Marjorie Hourd's valuable *The Education of the Poetic Spirit* (Heinemann, 1954).

compositions on 'My Favourite Hobby', 'Pets' or 'Our Garden'—and thousands and thousands of these things are turned out weekly—but rough, vigorous, lively, possibly un-grammatical and unrhythmical verse about—what? Anything and everything under the sun—it does not matter what, because a poem is always about itself: that is, the subject is subordinate to the treatment, the interest is in the handling of language.

I believe that some such revolution as this in teaching methods would do much to re-vitalize the attitude of our own language current in schools. It would also restore the prestige of poetry by enabling children to approach it not as the remote pursuit of impossibly gifted eccentrics, but as something they themselves were accustomed to practising, however inex-pertly. Why is it desirable that the prestige of poetry should be raised? This brings us back to the question which forms the title of this chapter.

Why teach poetry? For the reader who has followed so far, it is hardly necessary to give an answer. Yet sometimes the enthusiast for poetry is called upon to defend his position; and although he cannot hope to convert the entire opposition, he may persuade some and encourage others. The answer, I think, must begin with another question.

Why teach anything—anything, that is, beyond the quite elementary skills necessary for a member of a modern com-mercial community? The fact that man has a soul, as well as the mere instinct for survival, for comfort and physical well-being, is generally recognized. It would be truer to say, men have souls—or rather, each man has a soul. It is what is indi-vidual, distinctive and particular about him. He exists as a member of a community and as an individual; different nations order their political systems to give varying importance to these complementary, and in some ways rival, attributes of humanity. A liberal democracy, in comparison with an authoritarian state, places high value on the development of the individual. This is not the place to discuss social ethics, and in any case nobody seriously advocates any sort of education in

England which does not offer the fullest possibilities of self-expression to the individual, even at the risk of a tendency to anarchy. Those who complain that the present tendency to anarchy in Britain is dangerous and we need more social education, have a good and obvious case, but they would scarcely maintain that this is due to excessive concentration on the cultural side of education. On the contrary, the evidence tends to show that the bad member of society is also a bad individual; that the more fulfilled people are as individuals, the better citizens they will be.

The importance of the arts in the education of the individual is universally admitted, but the educational axiom that everyone is potentially and in some degree, an artist, does not somehow stretch to cover the word 'poet' as well. I would not be so bold as to say that everyone is a poet, or even a potential poet; but I would maintain that the spoken and the written word are at least as valuable media for potential self-fulfilment on the part of a great many people as line, colour, plastic shape, and musical sound.

Everybody uses language; no one has suggested that we can do without it. But the poverty of most people's verbal resources, both in speech and in writing, may be a sign of deficient emotional vitality. By 'emotional', I do not mean 'passionate'. I mean simply that man is not only a thinking, a seeing, a hearing, a working and a playing animal—he also feels. Language is the most universally available means of expressing feeling—it is also the most direct. There is a specialized quality about musical and graphic means of expressing emotion which is not present in the medium of language. Whatever specialized vocabularies poets may have adopted at different periods, language itself is unspecialized. It has one characteristic which limits it in a way that music and the plastic arts are not limited—it is regional; for this reason a nation's poetry is its most national—most personal—possession. No nation which claims to give its citizens a full cultural education can neglect its poetry. Among modern nations

England is in this respect in a peculiar position. The English language, for a number of reasons, is especially rich in poetic possibilities, and of all the arts poetry is in England of the most unequivocal supremacy. There is no need to labour the point. But it must be admitted that as a nation we are surprisingly indifferent to this part of the national inheritance. The English —and here I mean 'English-speaking', in whatever dialect— are a people of strong, though not at all times clearly articulate, feelings: nowhere have these feelings found a voice more memorably and more unmistakably than in our poetry. The poets have not always had a recognized place in society; but the best of what they have written has generally been regarded as characteristically English. If we let it become forgotten, we shall be the poorer.

CHAPTER 8

'THE HOLY INCANTATION'

In the introduction to these pages I referred to the evil of excessive inspirationalism in education. Yet ultimately we cannot do without inspiration: it is not a substitute for hard thinking and thoughtful experiment, for hammering out a solid technique of teaching. But all who are concerned with more than the day-to-day grind of class teaching must sometimes stop and ask, 'Where am I going? What is it for? Does this or that method or subject really further the ends of education?' We need a compass to steer by, even if we have no intention of trying to reach the magnetic north.

Before closing this book, then, I urge readers to study the following passages from an article contributed by D. H. Lawrence to an evening newspaper in 1928 under the title *Hymns in a Man's Life*. I make no apology for quoting at such length, because it is one of the best treatises on education ever written, and by far the best thing in these pages. It deserves to be quoted as the introduction to any prospectus for a teachers' training college.

Nothing is more difficult than to determine what a child takes in, and does not take in, of its environment and its teaching. This fact is brought home to me by the hymns which I learned as a child and never forgot. They mean to me almost more than the finest poetry, and they have for me a more permanent value, somehow or other.

It is almost shameful to confess that the poems which have meant most to me, like Wordsworth's *Ode to Immortality* and Keats's *Odes* and pieces of *Macbeth* or *As You Like It* or *Midsummer Night's Dream*, and Goethe's lyrics, such as *Uber allen Gipfeln ist Ruh*, and Verlaine's *Ayant poussé la porte qui chancelle*—

all these lovely poems which after all give the ultimate shape to one's life; all these lovely poems woven deep into a man's consciousness, are still not woven so deep in me as the rather banal Nonconformist hymns that penetrated through and through my childhood.

> Each gentle dove
> And sighing bough
> That makes the eve
> So fair to me
> Has something far
> Diviner now
> To draw me back
> To Galilee.
> O Galilee, sweet Galilee,
> Where Jesus loved so much to be,
> O Galilee, sweet Galilee,
> Come sing thy songs again to me!

To me the word Galilee has a wonderful sound. The Lake of Galilee! I don't want to know where it is. I never want to go to Palestine. Galilee is one of those lovely, glamorous worlds, not places, that exist in the golden haze of a child's half-formed imagination. And in my man's imagination it is just the same. It has been left untouched. With regard to the hymns which had such a profound influence on my childish consciousness, there has been no crystallizing out, no dwindling into actuality, no hardening into the commonplace. They are the same to my man's experience as they were to me nearly forty years ago.

The moon, perhaps, has shrunken a little. One has been forced to learn about orbits, eclipses, relative distances, dead worlds, craters of the moon, and so on. The crescent at evening still startles the soul with its delicate flashing. But the mind works, automatically and says: 'Ah, she is in her first quarter. She is all there, in spite of the fact that we see only this slim blade. The earth's shadow is over her.' And, willy-nilly, the intrusion of the mental processes dims the brilliance, the magic of the first apperception.

It is the same with all things. The sheer delight of a child's apperceptions is based on *wonder*; and deny it as we may, know-

ledge and wonder counteract one another. So that as knowledge
increases wonder decreases. We say again: Familiarity breeds
contempt. So that as we grow older, and become more familiar
with phenomena, we become more contemptuous of them. But
that is only partly true. It has taken some races of men thousands
of years to become contemptuous of the moon, and to the Hindu
the cow is still wondrous. It is not familiarity that breeds contempt: it is the assumption of knowledge. Anybody who looks
at the moon and says, 'I know all about that poor orb,' is, of
course, bored by the moon.

Now the great and fatal fruit of our civilization, which is a
civilization based on knowledge, and hostile to experience, is
boredom. All our wonderful education and learning is producing
a grand sum-total of boredom. Modern people are inwardly
thoroughly bored. Do as they may, they are bored.

They are bored because they experience nothing. And they
experience nothing because the wonder has gone out of them.
And when the wonder has gone out of a man he is dead. He is
henceforth only an insect.

When all comes to all, the most precious element in life is
wonder. Love is a great emotion, and power is power. But both
love and power are based on wonder. Love without wonder is
a sensational affair, and power without wonder is mere force and
compulsion. The one universal element in consciousness which is
fundamental to life is the element of wonder. You cannot help
feeling it in a bean as it starts to grow and pulls itself out of its
jacket. You cannot help feeling it in the glisten of the nucleus
of the amœba. You recognize it, willy-nilly, in an ant busily
tugging at a straw; in a rook, as it walks the frosty grass.

They all have their own obstinate will. But also they all live
with a sense of wonder. Plant consciousness, insect consciousness,
fish consciousness, animal consciousness, all are related by one
permanent element, which we may call the religious element
inherent in all life, even in a flea: the sense of wonder. This is our
sixth sense. And it is the *natural* religious sense.

Somebody says that mystery is nothing, because mystery is
something you don't know, and what you don't know is nothing
to you. But there is more than one way of knowing.

Even the real scientist works in the sense of wonder. The pity is, when he comes out of his laboratory he puts aside his wonder along with his apparatus, and tries to make it all perfectly didactic. Science in its true condition of wonder is as religious as any religion. But didactic science is as dead and boring as dogmatic religion. Both are wonderless and productive of boredom, endless boredom.

Now we come back to the hymns. They live and glisten in the depths of the man's consciousness in undimmed wonder, because they have not been subjected to any criticism or analysis. . . .

Lawrence here discusses a number of related topics, and I propose briefly to comment on some of them.

First, it might appear from a superficial reading that he was arguing in favour of bad poetry: what he says about the effect of hymns on the growth of his imagination in early childhood is apparently in opposition to what I wrote in a previous chapter on the necessity for giving children only good poetry. But this is not so.

Lawrence admits that the great poems (of Wordsworth, Keats, Shakespeare and the rest) 'give the ultimate shape to one's life'. But the Nonconformist hymns, he says, remained a more permanent possession because they were associated in his mind with the sense of wonder. Now Lawrence was an exceptional man and a writer—both of poetry and of prose. His poetic education did not end—indeed it may almost be said to have begun—when he left school. Dare we fill with bad poetry, even poetry charged with magic, the minds of children who will probably read no more poetry after they have left school? For it is poetry which the grown mind—the more critical mind—will reject as inadequate, and which may never be replaced, as it was in Lawrence's critical consciousness, by better poetry.

We know from his autobiographical poem *Piano* that hymns were of peculiar potency in Lawrence's early childhood because they were associated, not only with Chapel, but also with his mother. Can we doubt that if he had known no banal hymns, his imagination would have been stirred equally by better things, so that his adult mind would not have had to make a critical rejection of what had earlier excited him? Lawrence was forty-three when he wrote the article quoted above, and it is extraordinary that his early likes had still such a hold over him. Although I too was thrilled as a child by bad poems and sensational hymns, I cannot say that they retained a strong hold on my imagination after I had come to read better poems. But the fact that a man of forty-three could make such an admission is additional ground for giving young children only the best.

What Lawrence says about the primary importance of the sense of wonder seems to me undeniable and of the utmost significance. The more one ponders his words about 'the great and fatal fruit of our civilization'—boredom—the more one is convinced of the truth of his words. Of course he overstates and at one point contradicts himself, as was his custom: but his words have the kernel of truth. It has been proved in many departments of modern civilized life that the person who has many interests—that is, whose sense of curiosity or wonder remains alive—is physically healthy; there is no need to assume that 'wonder' always means 'rapture'; it may be something quiet and sustained. The old person who is bored is unhappy, a burden to himself and others; but to retain one's natural curiosity in old age is one of the most precious benefits obtainable.

Lawrence insists on the importance of what has been called 'primary experience'—the actual observation and contemplation of nature and human nature, actual participation in the experience of living. It is almost as if he were arguing in favour of the abandonment of all secondary experience—the experience of books, that is, and of art, and of knowledge in the widest sense. This is indeed a position he sometimes assumed, and it may be noticed in passing that there was here a fundamental inconsistency in his thinking. For he was himself a creative writer—a maker of poems and novels—and he must have known that such things add to the significance of life.

Indeed, he speaks here of the great poems giving 'the ultimate shape to one's life'. But this is a fallacy to which all romantics are prone—Wordsworth, for instance, who at one time used poetry for arguing against the kind of knowledge that comes from books. Nevertheless, it was essential to the thought of both Wordsworth and Lawrence that they should protest against the lack of balance in a civilization where knowledge is placed above primary experience.

Poetry can and does strengthen the sense of wonder if it is treated, not as a substitute for, but as an extension of experience. Children have observed nature, experienced love, fear, surprise; so have poets. Poetry is a form of interchange between minds. It was Keats's belief that poetry 'should strike the reader as a wording of his own highest thoughts, and appear almost a remembrance'. Primary experience is intensified by reading poetry, and the reading of poetry is vitalized by experience. I do not speak here of the unique experience which is to be had from certain poems and from them alone. No one could have experienced *Kubla Khan* before Coleridge wrote it; at the same time no one could respond to its magic—for it is magical in the sense of being a rite, a fertility rite—without at least partially 'understanding' it, that is, relating it to the known facts of experience, conscious, semi-conscious, or unconscious. Xanadu may indeed be to some readers what Galilee was to the young D. H. Lawrence, a pure intuition of ultimate mystery, about which there can be no rationalizing.

As to what Lawrence says of poetry and science, I find it difficult, despite the eloquence of a number of writers, to reconcile the two, at any rate as science is practised today. But that seems to me no reason whatever for throwing one or the other overboard. Life is full of irreconcilables. The contradictions between, say, peace and heroism, order and freedom, conviction and tolerance, ambition and contentment, passion and affection, self-fulfilment and altruism—these are inherent in life itself. So, it seems to me, is the contradiction between reason and irrationality. Science, whatever its original condition and inspiration, must be dedicated to reason. It proceeds by the rational exploration of nature, the ordering of all experience by the reason. Poetry, on the other hand, has a large and important element of unreason which, though certain ages may try to eradicate it, always springs up and reasserts itself.

> In sober mornings, doe not thou reherse
> The holy incantation of a verse.

Herrick, though an orthodox priest of the Anglican Church, recalled that poetry, even the pagan poetry of his *Hesperides*, was essentially religious and had a ritual quality which raised it out of the class of rational experience associated with 'sober mornings'.

Plato went further and insisted on the divine madness which inspires poets:

> For the authors of those great poems which we admire do not attain to excellence through the rules of any art, but utter their beautiful melodies of verse in a state of inspiration, and as it were, *possessed* by a spirit not their own. Thus the composers of lyrical poetry create those admired songs of theirs in a state of divine insanity, like the Corybantes, who lose all control over their reason in the enthusiasm of the sacred dance; and, during this supernatural possession, are excited to the rhythm and harmony which they communicate to men. . . . For whilst a man retains any portion of the thing called reason, he is utterly incompetent to produce poetry . . . But every rhapsodist or poet . . . is excellent in proportion to the extent of his participation in the divine influence, and the degree in which the Muse itself has descended on him.[1]

Shakespeare coupled the names of 'the lunatic, the lover, and the poet'. Many poets, for instance Clare, have written of the ecstasy of poetic possession when the rational world fades into non-existence while they are in its grip. Here is a statement by a Chinese poet, Po Chü-i, of the poetic frenzy.[2]

[1] Plato: *Ion* (Shelley's translation).
[2] *Madly Singing in the Mountains*, translated by Arthur Waley.

There is no one among men that has not a special failing:
And my failing consists in writing verses.
I have broken away from the thousand ties of life:
But this infirmity still remains behind.
Each time that I look at a fine lansdcape,
Each time that I meet a loved friend,
I raise my voice and recite a stanza of poetry
And am glad as though a God had crossed my path.
Ever since the day I was banished to Hsün-yang
Half my time I have lived among the hills.
And often, when I have finished a new poem,
Alone I climb the road to the Eastern Rock.
I lean my body on the banks of white stone:
I pull down with my hands a green cassia branch.
My mad singing startles the valleys and hills:
The apes and birds all come to peep.
Fearing to become a laughing-stock to the world,
I choose a place that is unfrequented by men.

Now whatever the origins of scientific inquiry in its pristine freshness of discovery, that is not the spirit in which it is taught. It does indeed appeal primarily to the imagination, but it works through the reason. We need both a rational and an irrational pole to the axis on which the human psyche revolves. However reasonably, then, we talk about poetry, however much we try to make it square with our sane and everyday experience, we have to remember that it is also a form of madness, of ecstasy or possession. Poetry, like love, is a form of lunacy; and there is an element of irrationality about all experience that has the quality of magic. Very few real pleasures are strictly reasonable.

Perhaps the most difficult thing of all, then, for a teacher of poetry to remember is that poetry is, after all, on the side of madness. He has to be so very reasonable, to discuss it so sanely, even to analyse it so scientifically, that he is in danger of forgetting that it is a 'holy incantation', a magical rite. If it were not, no nursery rhyme would have the power to hold the imagination and delight the ear of the infant, as it does.

Admittedly, the pages of this book have been sane enough. I wish it were otherwise; the habit of being reasonable is too strong, certainly for one who has been a teacher for nearly twenty years. But at the back of my mind all the time is a sense of the underlying madness of poetry, a madness which can help to keep us sane in a world where the demands upon our reason become more and more insistent. Our pleasures are sober, our holidays from routine are regulated by timetables, our conduct social and well-ordered. It is only in the world of fiction and make-believe that we can exercise with safety our instinct for disorder, violence and destruction—unless, that is, our boredom, like that of the later Romans, becomes so severe that we demand the spectacle of others killing themselves in public arenas or suffering personal disaster in all the glare of modern publicity.

I revert to *The Jumblies*, a saga of irrational heroism in a world of conventional sanity. 'Far and few' remains numinous to me—this was always one of the poems my mother enjoyed reading to us as children—much as the nonconformist incantations remained numinous to Lawrence. It is part of the function of poetry to persuade people that there is more in life than prudence, caution and sensible behaviour; that to go to sea in a sieve may be not only a heroic form of madness but also the way to adventure, excitement and discovery.

It may be that the best way to preserve for a class the magical element in poetry is, after all, simply to read it to them with all the skill and persuasiveness the teacher can command. I was, as a child, terrified by a supremely expressive recital of *Jabberwocky*; but it was, so to speak, a 'holy terror'. There was nothing morbid about it, and it did not trouble me at night. In later years it was a fine reading of *La Belle Dame Sans Merci* by Robert Harris and a deeply sympathetic reading of *The Idiot Boy* by Flora Robson that convinced me of the worth of these poems. My sense of the awfulness of the ballad of *Edward* is maintained by the ineffaceable memory of hearing John Laurie speak it on the radio ten years ago. It would be difficult to over-rate the power of the voice in conveying to an audience a sense of the poet's inspired utterance.

> And all should cry, Beware! Beware!
> His flashing eyes, his floating hair!
> Weave a circle round him thrice,
> And close your eyes with holy dread,
> For he on honey-dew hath fed,
> And drunk the milk of Paradise.

INDEX OF POETS AND POEMS

ALLINGHAM
The Fairies 37

ANONYMOUS BALLADS AND SONGS
Ballads 6, 11
The Death of Admiral Benbow 63–64, 78
Ding Dong Bell 31
The Farmer's Daughters 56–57
The Fox 38
The Golden Vanity 63–64
High Barbary 63–64
I saw a Peacock 54
John Cook's Mare 32
The Jolly Miller 49
Katherine Johnstone 79–80
Ladybird, Ladybird 34
Old Joe Braddle-um 57
Poor Old Horse 65, 79, 81
The Raggle-Taggle Gypsies 63–64
Robin Hood ballads 18, 80
Sir Eglamore 63
Sir Patrick Spens 6, 18, 23
Stormalong 81
Three Blind Mice 31
The Three Jovial Welshmen 56
When good King Arthur ruled the land 41–42
A Yankee Ship 23

BLAKE 7, 8, 65

BROWNING 78–79
How They Brought the Good News from Ghent
to Aix 7, 75, 78–79

BUNYAN
Pilgrim's Song 62

CLARE 65

COLERIDGE 18
The Ancient Mariner 72
Christabel 55
Kubla Khan 100, 104

COWPER
John Gilpin 7

DAVIES 65
The Rabbit 65, 82

DE LA MARE 7
Five Eyes 33
Nicholas Nye 55
Old Shellover 51
The Old Tailor 48–49
'Sooeep' 48–49

DOYLE
The Private of the Buffs 77

DRAYTON
Agincourt 77

GRAVES, ROBERT
A Cough 37

GRAY
Elegy 83

HARDY 7, 65
The Night of Trafalgar 77
Weathers 24, 50
We be the King's men 22

HAWKER
Song of the Western Men 14, 23

HERRICK 101

INGELOW, JEAN
The High Tide on the Coast of Lincolnshire 75

KEATS 11, 100
Meg Merrilies 47
A Naughty Boy 46–47
Ode to Autumn 25

LAWRENCE
Bat 69
Two Performing Elephants 81

LEAR 8, 18
The Jumblies 18, 53–54, 103
The Owl and the Pussycat 65

'LEWIS CARROLL'
Jabberwocky 45
The Lobster Quadrille 65

LONGFELLOW
Hiawatha 11
The Windmill 11

MACAULAY
Horatius 6

MARRYAT
The Old Navy 77

MASEFIELD, JOHN
Reynard the Fox 18

MILTON
Paradise Lost 72

NASHE
Spring 7

NEWBOLT
Admirals All 77–78
He Fell among Thieves 80

NOYES, ALFRED
Sherwood 80

PO CHÜ-I 101

REEVES, JAMES
A Thought 44

ROSSETTI, CHRISTINA 7

SANSOM, CLIVE
Clocks and Watches 36
Lightships 36

SCOTT
Young Lochinvar 79

SHAKESPEARE 7, 101
Blow, blow, thou Winter Wind 52
Macbeth 72
Romeo and Juliet 72
When Icicles hang by the Wall 49–50

SHELLEY
Ode to the West Wind 84
Ozymandias 16, 27, 83, 84

STEPHENS
The Snare 81

TENNYSON 7

WALEY, ARTHUR 8
At Fifteen I went with the Army 66–67
Madly Singing in the Mountains 102

WORDSWORTH 11

GENERAL INDEX

Biographical study 84
Choral Speech 19, 21–25, 38–41, 49–50, 54, 62–63
Comic verse 65
Counterfeit poetry 73–81
Critical and non-critical methods of study 17
Explanation of historical and geographical background,
    11, 15
Explanation of vocabulary 15–16, 52–53
Folk songs 31–33, 64
How long to study a poem in class 13, 28, 35
Individual reading aloud by children, 19, 20–21, 45–46
Introduction of a fresh poem 19–20
Lawrence, D. H., on poetic education 93–100
Learning by heart 27–28
Literary history 84–85
Liveliness in method 12–13
Mime 41
Nonsense verse 53–55, 65
Nursery rhymes 30–31
Original verse by children 55–58, 66–70, 85–86, 91–92
Paraphrase as an approach to poetry 82
Pictorial illustration 17, 49, 55
Plato 101
Politics and education 92–93
Preparation of material 14
Propaganda in poetry 81–83
'Pulling a poem to pieces' 25
Reading aloud by teacher 18, 46
Reading round the class 20–21
Science and poetry 100
Silent reading by class 18
'Sing-song' in class reading 33
Speech rhymes 35
Speech training 35, 43, 61–62
Taste in education 73–74
Technical study of poetry 83–84
Variety in method 12–13